Praying God's Word

A Handbook of Scriptural Prayers
& Faith Confessions

Dr. Hazel Hill

Copyright © 1995 – Dr. Hazel Hill
Revised Printing 2015
Printed in Canada
International Standard Book Number 978-0-920567-60-9
Victory Churches International
10623 West Valley Road SW
Calgary, AB T3B 5T2
Website: www.victoryint.org

Unless otherwise indicated, all Scripture quotations are taken from the New King James and Amplified versions of the Bible.

For Worldwide Distribution

Endorsement

I am so thankful to be alive and to be able to bring you a message of hope. That is what Jesus is – hope! I feel like the Psalmist David, who said, "O Lord... I pleaded with you and you gave me my health again. You brought me back from the brink of the grave, from death itself, and here I am alive!" (Psalm 30:2-3 TLB)

The Word of God is extremely important to people who are fighting any spiritual battles, for often it is the only hope they have. I know I would have died if it had not been for the Word of God, but I had been taught the truth from God's Word. God said, "My people are destroyed for lack of knowledge." (Hosea 4:6) Many people do not have knowledge of the Word of God or know it is God's will for them to have victory in their lives. God does not want you to be defeated. He wants you to live and declare the works of the Lord!

That is why I highly recommend this book by Hazel Hill, that will aptly teach you to Pray God's Word.

Dodie Osteen

Dodie Osteen

INTRODUCTION

What was the reason for the victorious power that Jesus displayed in prayer? Not only was Jesus the living Word but He prayed the Word. You can experience this same authority over every circumstance and have victory in answered prayer, by following His example: **Pray the Word.**

This book contains a collection of powerful Word prayers adapted from the Word of God. Many of the prayers may contain statements describing events that are not taking place in your life, your home, or your church. Don't let this hinder your prayers. Remember, Abraham was called faithful and righteous because he called those things which 'be not as though they were' (Rom 4:17-18). Your confession of the scriptures, in faith, will bring about those things for which you are praying.

The Word of God is quick and powerful and sharper than any two-edged sword (Heb 4:12). It is alive and active. God Himself watches over His Word to perform it, or to make sure it comes to pass (Jer 1:12). God's Word shall never return void but always accomplishes that for which it is sent (Isa. 55:11). Even the angels hearken to His word and are ministering spirits sent to minister for us (Ps 105:20; Heb 1:14). I Corinthians 14:15 says, "I will pray in the spirit (which means in our heavenly language – tongues) and I will pray with the understanding also."

When I pray, I like to pray the Word and then pray in tongues for a while as I wait on the Lord Jesus to see if He wants me to pray further for the area at hand. Very often He will drop things into my spirit. I then pray according to the understanding He has given me. Then back to tongues and then the Word again.

This is a very effective way to pray. Always have one ear tuned to the Holy Spirit in you as you pray. Develop a hearing ear. Don't be a parrot, simply regurgitating the Word of God from your mind. It is to be prayed in faith - believing. Remember, "Faith comes by hearing and hearing by the Word of God" and faith is of the heart. When you have stored all the wonderful Word contained in this book in your heart, give the book to a friend and allow the Lord to bring all these scriptures to your remembrance as needed in prayer. Ask the Holy Spirit to freshly anoint your intercession.

Always pray specifically. Perhaps use a prayer journal and write down whom and what you are praying for, as well as your scriptural basIs Then go back over your journal from time to time and thank the Lord for the answers. Don't hesitate to continue to bring an issue before the Lord more than once. "The earnest (heartfelt continued) prayer of a righteous man makes tremendous power available (dynamic in its working)" James 5:16 (Amp)

I love you and will be praying for you.

INDEX OF PRAYERS

Chapter One

PRAYERS FOR OUR NATION AND THE CHURCH

Prayer For Our Nation

"Therefore I exhort first of all that supplications, prayers, intercessions, and giving of thanks be made for all men, for kings and all who are in authority, that we may lead a quiet and peaceable life in all godliness and reverence."
2 Tim 2:1-2

Father, we come to You today and pray for our Nation and its leaders. We know that Proverbs 29:2 says, "When the righteous are in authority, the people rejoice; But when a wicked man rules, the people groan." Therefore, we cry unto You to move on their hearts, save their souls or remove them from office, in Jesus' Name. Let light shine in the darkness of their minds and may they come to their right mind and escape out of the snare the devil has set for us all.

Lord we know that king's hearts are in the hand of the Lord and You turn them wherever You like, just as the water course.

Therefore, today we pray that You take the hearts of those who rule over us and turn their hearts toward righteousness and wisdom from above. Visit them in the night hours in dreams and visions. Show up with writing on their walls or a personal visit from Jesus, that they may awake out of their sleep and rule the country with Your wisdom and the right hand of Your righteousness.

Send a vision or dream as You did to Pharaoh that only a man of God could interpret. Or, as You did to King Nebuchadnezzar, even if it makes them sick and unable to eat or sleep. Speak to our leaders in Jesus' Name we pray!

Write Your wisdom on their walls as You did to get the King's attention in Daniel 5.

Lord, we humble ourselves before You this day. We are Your people and we are called by Your Name. We pray and seek Your face, and turn from our wicked ways. We know then that You will hear from heaven, and will forgive our sin and heal our land.

Forgive the sins of this nation Father. The abortion, the moral decay and the wickedness of the hearts of people; this nation's disrespect for You and the dishonour this nation has brought You. We repent on behalf of this nation in Jesus' Name.

Lord have mercy on us and deliver us from terrorists and the evil men and woman that come to destroy our land, for You have ordained peace for us in Jesus' Name.

Yes, Lord, although others reject Israel we will not! We will pray for the peace of Jerusalem and stand on guard for You in this land, in Jesus' Name.

Study: 2 Tim 2: 1-2; Prov 29:2; Pro 21:1; Dan 4; Dan 5; 2 Chron 7:14

Leaders of Our Nation

Paul exhorts us in I Timothy 2:1-3 to pray *"first of all for all who are in authority, that we may lead a quiet and peaceable life in all godliness and honesty. For this is good and acceptable in the sight of God our Savior."*

Father God, the hearts of our leaders are in Your hands even as the water courses; and You turn them whichever way You will. Therefore, I pray that skillful and godly wisdom will enter the hearts of our leaders; that the knowledge of God be pleasant to them. I pray that discretion will watch over them and understanding keep them; to deliver them from the evil way and from evil men and women – from lying persons who speak perverse things, who forsake the paths of righteousness to walk in the ways of darkness. Deliver them from evil doers and terrorists who have come to steal, kill and destroy.

I pray that the Spirit of the Lord would rest upon our leaders; a spirit of wisdom and understanding, the spirit of counsel and might, the spirit of knowledge and of the fear of the Lord. Make our leaders of quick understanding so that their delight shall be in the fear of the Lord. May they not judge by the sight of their eyes, neither decide by the hearing of their ears; but with righteousness and justice let them judge the poor, and the downtrodden of the earth. Let righteousness be the girdle of their waist, and faithfulness the girdle of their loins.

Study: Prov 21:1; Prov 2:10-16; Is 11:2-5 (Amp.)

Israel & The Middle East

Pray for the peace of Jerusalem: "May they prosper who love you. Peace be within your walls, Prosperity within your palaces." Ps 122:6

Father, I pray for the peace of Jerusalem, that peace would be within her walls and prosperity within her palaces. I pray for the Middle East that they might be saved and that their zeal would be according to the knowledge of the truth. Redeem Israel, O God, out of all her troubles. Remember Your covenant to her, O God, and confirm it as an everlasting covenant. We pray for peace in The Middle East.

I say that Israel continually hopes in You and experiences Your mercy and plenteous redemption. Gather the outcasts of Israel unto Yourself. Let Your lovingkindness and great goodness be bestowed upon Israel, for You are merciful and full of compassion.

For Jerusalem's sake, I will give You no rest, until her righteousness goes forth as brightness and salvation as a lamp that burns. Build up Jerusalem and let her warfare be accomplished and her iniquity be pardoned. I pray that neither weeping nor crying will be heard in her streets, but that she would rejoice and her people be a joy unto You, in Jesus' Name.

Study: Ps 122:6,7; Rom 10:1-2; Ps 25:22; Ps 105:10; Ps 130:7; Is 63:7; Is 62:1; Is 40:2,9; Is 65:19

Pastors

Finally, brethren, pray for us, that the word of the Lord may run swiftly and be glorified, just as it is with you. 2 Thes 3:1

Thank You Father, for giving us pastors after Your own heart, who feed us with knowledge and understanding. Thank You that the pastors You have placed over us feed us, so that we fear no more, nor are dismayed, nor are we lacking in any way. I pray that You would open for them a door of utterance that they may speak the Word boldly; that the Word of God may run swiftly and be glorified; that they may be delivered from unreasonable and wicked men and women, and the antagonists. Surround them with favor as with a shield.

Thank You Father, for watching over our pastors and their families, their marriages, their homes and possessions, for giving Your angels charge over them to keep them in all their ways. I confess for them that no evil befalls them, and no plague comes near them. Thank You that they attend to Your words, they incline their ears unto Your sayings, they do not let them depart from before their eyes, and they keep them in the midst of their hearts. Your Word is life unto them and health to all their flesh.

I pray that our pastors will not let Your Word depart out of their mouth, but they will meditate in it day and night, that they may observe to do according to all that is written in it, thus they will make their way prosperous, and they shall have good success. Lord, give our pastors faithful and mighty intercessors, through the Lord Jesus Christ, and through the love of the Spirit, who will always strive together with them in prayers, in Jesus' Name.

Study: Jer 23:4; Eph 6:19; 2 Thess 3:1,2; Ps 5:12; Ps 91:9-10; Prov 4:20-22; Josh 1:8; Rom 15:30

Missionaries

That Your way may be known on earth, Your salvation among all nations.
Ps 67:2

Father, I lift up to You our missionaries, _____. I pray that they may be filled with the knowledge of Your will in all wisdom and spiritual understanding, that they may walk worthy of You unto all pleasing, being fruitful in every good work and increasing in the knowledge of God. Thank You that because they abide in You they bring forth much fruit and their fruit remains.

Thank You for giving Your angels charge over _____ to keep them in all their ways of service and obedience so that no evil befalls them and no plague comes near them. Thank You that Jesus took their infirmities and bore their sicknesses and by His stripes they were healed. Thank You that even if they eat any deadly thing, it shall not hurt them.

Thank You Father, for supplying all their needs according to Your riches in glory, for making all grace abound toward them so that they always have all sufficiency in all things and abound to every good work. Thank You that they teach others to give and prosper, even in the poorest of nations.

I pray for their marriage Lord, and say that they are of one mind, having compassion for each other, loving as brethren, being tender and courteous to one another. I pray for their children that You would watch over and keep them. I pray that they would be taught of the Lord, and their peace would be great. Thank You that their whole family stands firm in united spirit and purpose, striving side by side and contending with a single mind for the faith of the gospel.

I pray that You would give them doors of utterance, that Your Word would have free course and be glorified. I pray that they would be delivered from unreasonable and wicked people, in Jesus' Name.

Study: Col 1:9-10; John 15:16; Ps 91:9-10; Matt 8:17; 1 Pet. 2:24; Mark 16:18; Philem. 4:19; 2 Cor 9:8; 1 Pet. 3:8,9; Is 54:13; Phil 1:27; Eph 6:19; Col 4:3-4; 2 Thess 3:1,2

Local Church

I write so that you may know how you ought to conduct yourself in the house of God, which is the church of the living God, the pillar and ground of the truth. 1 Tim 3:15

Father God, we thank You that our congregation is filled with the spirit of wisdom and revelation in the knowledge of You. They are fulfilling Your perfect purpose and plan for their lives.

They hear the voice of the Good Shepherd and the voice of a stranger they will not follow. We pray that the Spirit of wisdom, knowledge, counsel, might, and understanding will guide them in every meeting, activity and conversation they engage in. We thank You that they give themselves continually to prayer, and to the ministry of the Word.

We thank You that they are protected from all hurt, harm, danger and accidents. They are the redeemed of the Lord and in covenant with Jehovah God, therefore sickness, disease, poverty, lack, fear and oppression have no power over them. They walk in divine health and are physically fit. Their souls prosper because they meditate in God's Word day and night.

No weapon that is formed against them shall prosper and every lying tongue raised against them shall be silenced. Every business deal works to their favor and advantage, and Your blessings overtake them because they hearken diligently unto the voice of the Lord their God, and they are faithful in their tithes and offerings to their local church.

We cancel every attack of the wicked one to bring deception, distractions, hindrances and temptations into their lives. Devil, you are bound and have no authority over our families, possessions, or us. We cover our congregation with the blood of Jesus, and release the angels of God to minister to them and bring them into God's best every day of their lives.

We thank You that our church is of one heart in one accord, and is enjoying the days of heaven upon the earth. Their seed is mighty upon the earth and blessed. Wealth and riches are in their homes. They fellowship with people of like precious faith, and have set a new standard of excellence for the body of Christ. They work together with their pastors, submitting themselves to godly leadership. In Jesus' Name, amen.

Study: Eph 1:17,18; Col 1:9; John 10:27; Is 11:2; Ps91: 9,10; Ex 6: 3-7; Ex 23:25; John 1:2; Ps 119:148; Is 54:17; Ps 103:5; Deut 28:2; Mal.3:10; Luke 10:19; Matt 18:18; Ex 12:1-13; Phil 2:2; Ps 37:26; 2Pet 1:1; Eph 5:21;

Unity

Let your conduct be worthy of the gospel of Christ, so that whether I come and see you or am absent, I may hear of your affairs, that you stand fast in one spirit, with one mind striving together for the faith. Phil 1:27

Heavenly Father, in the Name of Jesus, I thank You for a spirit of unity in the Body of Christ, and in our local church. I pray that we would all speak the same thing, and there would be no divisions among us, but we would be perfectly joined together in the same mind and in the same judgment. It is a good and pleasant thing that we as brethren dwell and work together in unity. We strive earnestly to guard and keep the harmony and the unity of the Spirit in the bond of peace.

I pray that we increase, excel and overflow in love for one another and for all people. Thank You that Your love in us flows fervently from pure hearts toward one another. I pray that we would be of the same mind (united in spirit), working with and loving one another as brethren, compassionate, courteous, tenderhearted and humble.

Father, I pray also that as we continue to walk in the light as You are in the light, that we would have unbroken fellowship with one another and be cleansed from all sin and unrighteousness by the blood of Jesus. I pray that the spirit of unity would knit Your body together so that we would bring You glory and the world would believe. In Jesus' Name!

Study: 1 Cor 1:10; Ps 133:1; Eph 4:3; 1 Thes 3:12; 1 Pet 1:22; 1 Pet 3:8; 1 John 1:7; Eph 4:16

The Power Of Teamwork

I say to you that if two of you agree on earth concerning anything that they ask, it will be done for them by My Father in heaven. For where two or three are gathered together in My Name, I am there in the midst of them. Matt 18:19-20

Father, we know that You have ordained mankind to work in teams. I thank You that we are stronger working together then apart. Five of us working together in unity will chase a hundred enemies and one hundred of us working together in unity shall put ten thousand to flight. Two are better than one, because they have a good reward for their labor. For if one falls, the one will lift his fellow, but woe to him that is alone when he falls, for he has no one to help him up. A threefold cord is not quickly broken. If two of us agree on earth as touching anything that we ask, it shall be done for us of our Father which is in heaven. We know You are in our midst when two or three of us gather together in Your Name.

We will not let division or strife separate us for a kingdom divided against itself will not stand.

Thank You Lord that You teach me to work as a team member in my home, my church, at work and at play in Jesus' Name. Amen

Study: Lev 26:8, Ecc 4:9-12, Matt 18:19-20, Matt 12:25

Paul's Ephesians Prayer

Father of Glory, I pray that You would grant unto me the spirit of wisdom and revelation, a spirit of insight into mysteries and secrets in the deep and intimate knowledge of You. Flood the eyes of my heart with light, so that I can know and understand the hope to which You have called me, the richness of Your glorious inheritance in the immeasurable and unlimited and surpassing greatness of Your power in and for us who believe.

Study: Eph 1:17-19

Paul's Philippians Prayer

Holy Father, I pray that my love may abound yet more and more and extend to its fullest development in knowledge and all keen insight, that is, that my love may display itself in greater depth of acquaintance and more comprehensive discernment. Thank You Father, that I learn to sense what is vital, and approve and prize what is excellent and of real value, recognizing the highest and the best, and distinguishing the moral differences. I pray that I may be untainted, pure, unerring and blameless, that with my heart sincere and certain, I may approach the day of Christ, not stumbling nor causing others to stumble. I pray that I may abound in and be filled with the fruits of righteousness, to Your honor Lord and praise, that Your glory may be both manifested and recognized. In Jesus' Name.

Paul's Colossians Prayer

Gracious Father, I pray that I may be filled with the full, deep, and clear knowledge of Your will in all spiritual wisdom (that is, in comprehensive insight into the ways and purposes of God) and in understanding and discernment of spiritual things. I pray that I would walk (live and conduct myself) in a manner worthy of You, fully pleasing to You. I pray that I would bear fruit in every good work and steadily grow and increase in the knowledge of God with fuller, deeper, and clearer insight, acquaintance and recognition. I pray that I may be invigorated and strengthened with all power, according to the might of Your glory, that I may exercise every kind of endurance and patience, perseverance and forbearance with joy. I thank You for making me fit to share the inheritance of the saints in light.

David's Psalm 119 Prayer

My Father, I pray that You remove from me the way of falsehood and unfaithfulness to You, and graciously impart Your law to me. I have chosen the way of truth and faithfulness; I have set Your ordinances before me. I cleave to Your testimonies. O Lord, do not let me be put to shame. I will not merely walk, but run in the way of Your commandments, when You give me a willing heart. Teach me, O Lord, the way of Your statutes, and I will keep them steadfastly unto the end. Give me understanding, that I may keep Your law; yes, I will observe it with my whole heart. Make me to go in the path of Your commandments, for in them do I delight. Incline my heart to Your testimonies, and not to covetousness, robbery, sensuality and unworthy riches. Turn away my eyes from beholding vanity; and restore me to vigorous life and health. Establish Your Word in me and confirm Your promises as I devotedly worship You. I long for Your precepts; in Your righteousness give me renewed life. Let Your mercies and lovingkindness come also to me, that is salvation (healing, preservation, safety, soundness and deliverance), according to Your promise.

To Be an Intercessor

Now it came to pass, as He was praying in a certain place, when He ceased, that one of His disciples said to Him, "Lord, teach us to pray, as John also taught his disciples. Luke 11:1

Father, I desire to become an artful intercessor. Oh that my head were waters and my eyes a fountain of tears, that I might weep day and night for the lost, the bound, the oppressed and unrepentant. Grant unto me, Father, that I would be a clean vessel, set apart and useful for honorable and noble purposes, consecrated and profitable to You Master, fit and ready for any work. I pray that I would be a skillful and wise person, able to express grief and sorrow, to wail mournful cries and lamentation as I am moved with compassion on behalf of others. Father, I pray that I would, by Your Holy Spirit, travail and give birth to the lost so that repentance would be granted them. May I be faithful to travail until Christ is completely and permanently formed within the young Christians. I lay down my life to bring deliverance for the bound and oppressed, and healing for the sick in mind and body. I cry unto You Lord, that repentance be granted to the backsliders, that their eyes run with tears.

I desire to continue in supplications and prayers night and day, to never hold my peace nor give You rest until You establish and make Your people a praise in the earth. I will pray always with all prayer and supplication in the Spirit and watch thereunto with all perseverance and supplication for all saints as You strengthen me.

Thank You my Father, for releasing me now to intercede on behalf of Your people. I yield myself to You, Holy Spirit.

Study: Is 59:16; Jer 9:1; 2 Tim 2:21,25; Gal 4:19; Is 58:6; Jer 14:17; Is 62:6; Eph 6:18

Spiritual Warfare Prayer

The LORD shall go forth like a mighty man; He shall stir up His zeal like a man of war. He shall cry out, yes, shout aloud; He shall prevail against His enemies. Isa 42:13

Father, in Jesus Name, by faith, I put on the whole armour of God so that I may stand against the wiles, strategy, plots and schemes of the devil. I put on the helmet of hope and salvation to protect my mind from the deceitful thoughts of the enemy, that the mind which is in Christ Jesus may be in me also. I put on the breastplate of righteousness, always remembering that I am the righteousness of God in Christ Jesus.

I put on the girdle or belt of truth, the truth and integrity and the holiness of God. I put on the sandals of the Gospel of peace, always endeavouring to walk in the peace that passes all understanding. Above all, I take up the shield of faith to quench every fiery dart, arrow, spear, and missile the enemy shoots my way. I take up the sword of the Spirit which is the Word of God that is alive and powerful, sharper than any two-edged sword. I say that the Word going out of my mouth is just as powerful as it is going out of the mouth of God, because I speak only His Words. His Word will not return void or empty and will prosper in the thing for which I send it, in Jesus' Name. Lord help me to always remember to pray for all the people You lay on my heart with all supplications in the Spirit, being watchful at all times. You have made a hedge around me and around my household, and around all that I have on every side. You have blessed the work of my hands, and my possessions will increase in the land.

Study: Eph 6:10-18, 2 Cor 5:21, Heb 4:12, Is 55:11, Job 1:10, Ex 15:3, Ps 144

Prayer For Spiritual Protection

My help comes from the LORD, Who made heaven and earth. He will not allow your foot to be moved; He who keeps you will not slumber.
Ps 121:2-3

Father, In the Name of Jesus, I ask You to keep the same hedge of protection around me, my family, my mind, my heart and emotions, as it is written in Job 1:10.

Thank You Lord that the angel of the LORD encamps round about me because I reverently fear You and You deliver me in every situation. For You shall give Your angels charge over me, to keep me in all of my ways of service and obedience. They shall bear me up in their hands, lest I dash my foot against a stone. Father, in Jesus' Name, I ask You to keep an encampment of Your powerful angels around me 24 hours a day.

Thank You Lord that these angels are all ministering spirits sent forth to minister for those who will inherit salvation. I thank You Lord this includes me.
Father, in Jesus' Name, I ask You to send a host of ministering angels to minister to my hurts, needs, pain and infirmities, strengthening me today in every way.

Thank You Lord that Your glory is my rear guard and You will put a wall of fire around me to insulate me from and assaults of the devil. Then my light shall break forth like the morning and Your healing power will spring forth speedily.
I will not be afraid, for You Lord are my shield and You are my exceedingly great reward.

For though I walk in the flesh, I do not war according to the flesh. For the weapons of our warfare are not carnal, but mighty in God for pulling down strongholds, casting down arguments and every high thing that exalts itself against the knowledge of God, bringing every thought into captivity to the obedience of Christ. I cast down all imaginations and any high thing that exalts itself against the knowledge of God, bringing every one of my thoughts into captivity to the obedience of Christ, in Jesus' Name.

I say that no weapon formed against me shall prosper, and every tongue which rises in judgment against me shall be condemned. This is the heritage of the servants of the Lord and our righteousness is of You, Oh Lord.

Study: Job 1:10, Ps 34:7, Ps 91:11-12, Heb 1:14, Is 52:12; 58:8, 1 Cor 10:3-5

I will praise You, O LORD, with my whole heart; I will tell of all Your marvelous works. {2} I will be glad and rejoice in You; I will sing praise to Your Name, O Most High. Psalm 9:1-2

I will bless the LORD who has given me counsel; My heart also instructs me in the night seasons. Psalm 16:7

I will praise the LORD according to His righteousness, And will sing praise to the Name of the LORD Most High. Psalm 7:17

I will love You, O LORD, my strength. {2} The LORD is my rock and my fortress and my deliverer; My God, my strength, in whom I will trust; My shield and the horn of my salvation, my stronghold. {3} I will call upon the LORD, who is worthy to be praised; So shall I be saved from my enemies. Psalm 18:1-3

And now my head shall be lifted up above my enemies all around me; Therefore I will offer sacrifices of joy in His tabernacle; I will sing, yes, I will sing praises to the LORD. Psalm 27:6

When You said, "Seek My face," My heart said to You, "Your face, LORD, I will seek." Psalm 27:8

I will bless the LORD at all times; His praise shall continually be in my mouth. Psalm 34:1

I acknowledged my sin to You, And my iniquity I have not hidden. I said, "I will confess my transgressions to the LORD," And You forgave the iniquity of my sin. Psalm 32:5

Chapter Two

GENERAL PRAYERS

Praise

Enter into His gates with thanksgiving, And into His courts with praise. Be thankful to Him, and bless His Name. Ps 100:4

O mighty Father, all greatness, power, victory and majesty are Yours. All that is in heaven and earth is Yours. You are exalted as Ruler over all things. As I sing praises to You, I thank You for setting ambushments against my enemies. I praise You according to Your righteousness.

I will sing praises to Your Name. With my whole heart I praise You, showing forth all Your marvelous works. I will be glad and rejoice in You. I will sing praise to Your Name, O Most High.

Let not the wise man glory in his wisdom. Let not the mighty man glory in his might. Nor let the rich man glory in his riches; but let him who glories glory in this, that he understands and knows You, for You are the LORD, exercising loving-kindness, judgment and righteousness in the earth. The Lord is gracious and full of compassion, slow to anger and great in mercy. The Lord is good to all, and His tender mercies are over all His works. The Lord is near to all who call upon Him, to all who call upon Him in truth. He will fulfill the desire of those who fear Him.

I will bless the Lord at all times; His praise shall continually be in mouth. My soul shall make its boast in the Lord; the humble shall hear of it and be glad. Oh, magnify the Lord with me, and let us exalt His Name together. Let everything that has breath praise the Lord. Praise ye the Lord!

Study: 1 Chr 29:11, 13; 2 Chr 20:22; Ps 7:17; Ps 9:1; Jer 9:23,24; Ps 145:8-9, 18-19; Ps 34:1-3; Ps 150:6

Right Pathway for Your Family

You will show me the path of life; In Your presence is fullness of joy; At Your right hand are pleasures forevermore. Ps 16:11

Thank You Father, in Jesus' Name, that the Word of God leads us, keeps us when we sleep and talks to us when we awaken. Your Word is a lamp unto our feet and a light unto our path. Lead us in the pathway of righteousness for Your Name's sake. Father, I thank You that You lead my family and me in the way that we should go and counsel us with Your eye.

My family and I hear the voice of the Good Shepherd and the voice of a stranger we will not hear. We are sons and daughters of God who are led by the Spirit of God. Thank You that the Spirit of truth teaches us and leads us into all truth. Our pathway is like the light of dawn that shines more brightly and clearly until it reaches its full strength and glory unto that perfect day. In our pathway is life and not death. We are God's own handiwork, recreated in Christ Jesus that we may do the works which You Father, planned beforehand. We take paths which You have prearranged and made ready.

Thank You for sending Your angels before us to bring us to the place which You have prepared for us. In Jesus' Name.

Study: Prov 6:22-23; Ps 119: 105; Ps 23:3; Ps 32:8; John 10:3-5; Rom 8:14; Prov 4:18; Eph 2:10; John 16:13; Ex 23:20

Wisdom and Guidance

Wisdom is the principal thing; Therefore get wisdom. And in all your getting, get understanding. Pro 4:7

I thank You Father, that the Spirit of truth has come and now abides in me. He teaches me all things and guides me into all truth. I will not let mercy and kindness and truth forsake me; but I will bind them about my neck, and write them upon the tables of my heart. Therefore, I will find favor, good understanding and high esteem in the sight of God and man. I lean on, trust and am confident in You Lord. With all my heart and mind I will trust You and will not rely on my own understanding. In all my ways I will recognize and acknowledge You. I know that You will direct and make straight and plain my paths. I will not be wise in my own eyes but I will reverently fear and worship You and turn entirely away from evil.

Thank You Lord, that You are perfecting that which concerns me. Father of glory, grant unto me a spirit of wisdom and revelation of insight, into mysteries and secrets in the deep and intimate knowledge of You, having the eyes of my heart flooded with light, so that I can know and understand the hope to which You have called me, and know the glorious riches of my inheritance. I thank You, Father, that I am born of God, and I have world-overcoming faith residing on the inside of me. Greater is He that is in me, than he that is in the world.

Father God, thank You that You have stored away sound and godly wisdom for me because I am righteous through Christ. I receive Your wisdom from on high now. Thanks be unto God, who always causes me to triumph in Christ Jesus our Lord and Master.

Study: John 16:13; Prov 3:3-7; Ps 138:8; Eph 1:17-18; 1 John 5:4-5; Prov 2:7 (Amp.); 2 Cor 2:14

Protection from Satan's Weapons

No weapon formed against you shall prosper, And every tongue which rises against you in judgment you shall condemn. This is the heritage of the servants of the LORD. Is 54:17

Thank You Father, that no weapon formed against me shall prosper and every tongue that shall rise up against me in judgment shall be shown to be in the wrong. For this security and triumph over opposition is the heritage of the servants of the Lord. As my ways please You, You will make even my enemies to be at peace with me.

Thank You that You bring the counsel of the enemy to naught and make his thoughts and plans of no effect. Many evils may confront me, but the Lord delivers me out of them all. I say of the Lord, "He is my refuge and my fortress, my God in whom I trust." Lord, You deliver me from every snare and trap of the enemy. You redeem the life of Your servants. If God be for us, who can succeed against us? I am never utterly cast down for You uphold me with Your right arm. I will tread on serpents and scorpions and over all the power of the enemy, and nothing shall by any means hurt me.

Study: Is 54:17; Prov 16:7; Ps 33:10; Ps 34:19; Ps 91:2-3; Rom 8:31; Ps 37:24; Luke 10:19

Strength and Youth

But those who wait on the LORD shall renew their strength; they shall mount up with wings like eagles, they shall run and not be weary, they shall walk and not faint. Is 40:31

Thank You Father, that I have strength for all things through Christ. I am ready for anything and equal to everything through Jesus who infuses His strength into me. I am strengthened and reinforced with mighty power in the inner man by the Holy Spirit. Thank You Lord that You keep me from stumbling or falling and present me unblemished, blameless and faultless before the presence of Your glory with unspeakable delight. Though I feel weak, I say, "I am strong!"

You renew my strength as I wait upon You, so that I am able to mount up with wings as an eagle. I run and do not get weary; I walk and do not faint. The same Spirit who raised Christ from the dead dwells in me and quickens my mortal body. He quickens my immune system, my metabolism, my hearing and my eyesight, my reflexes and my memory and all the functions of my body. Thank You for satisfying my mouth with good things so that my youth and strength are renewed like the eagle's. In Jesus' Name.

Study: Phil 4:13; Eph 3:16; Jude 24; Joel 3:10; Is 40:31; Rom 8:11; Ps 103:5

Forgiveness

And whenever you stand praying, if you have anything against anyone, forgive him, that your Father in heaven may also forgive you your trespasses. Mk 11:25

Father, in the Name of Jesus, I make a fresh commitment to You to live in peace and harmony, not only with the Body of Christ, but also with my family, friends, neighbors and associates. I let go of all bitterness, resentment, envy, strife, and unkindness in any form. I give no place to Satan in Jesus' Name. I ask for Your forgiveness and receive it by faith, having assurance that I am cleansed from all unrighteousness through the blood of Jesus.

I ask You to forgive and release all who have wronged or hurt me. I also forgive and release them. Deal with them in Your mercy and lovingkindness. I purpose to walk in love, to seek peace, to live in agreement, and to conduct myself toward others in a manner that is pleasing to You.

Study: Eph 4:31; 1 John 1:9, Matt 18:28-35

Guidance

When you roam, they will lead you; When you sleep, they will keep you; And when you awake, they will speak with you. For the commandment is a lamp, And the law a light. Pro 6:22-23

Father, I pray You will fill me with the knowledge of Your will in all wisdom and spiritual understanding that I may be fruitful in every good work. I ask You to order my steps according to Your Word and let no iniquity have dominion over me. As I plan my way I look to You to direct my steps and make them sure. Whatever plans may be in my mind, I ask that it be Your purpose for me that will stand.

You are my Good Shepherd and I know Your voice and will not follow another. I trust in You with all my heart and do not rely upon my own insight or understanding. In all my ways I acknowledge You as my Lord. Daily You direct my steps, delivering me from any and all hidden dangers and traps set by the enemy. I thank You for the ministry of Your angels, who have been given charge over me to guard and protect me in all my ways of service and obedience, to keep me in the way and bring me to the place You have prepared for me. Praise Your mighty Name!

Study: Col 1:9; Ps 119:133; Prov 19:21; John 10:4-5; Prov 3:5-6; Ps 91:11; Ex 23:20, Is 30:21

Godly Speech

Let your speech always be with grace, seasoned with salt, that you may know
how you ought to answer each one. Col 4:6

Father, let my speech at all times be gracious (pleasant and winsome), seasoned with salt, so that I may never be at a loss to know how I ought to answer anyone who puts a question to me.

O Lord, help me to speak excellent and princely things and let the opening of my lips be for right things. Let my mouth utter truth and may all the words of my mouth be righteous. May there be nothing contrary to truth or crooked in them. For the words of the pure are pleasing words to You Father, and from the fruit of my lips I shall be satisfied with good.

Father, I will keep my heart with all vigilance and guard it, for out of it flow the springs of life. I will put away false and dishonest speech, and willful and contrary talk I will put far from me. I pray that I might exercise proper discretion and that my lips may guard and keep knowledge. For the mouth of an uncompromisingly righteous man is a well of life. Filthiness, foolish talking or jesting which is not convenient is put far from me. I will let no corrupt communication proceed out of my mouth, but that which is good for edification, that it may minister grace to the hearers.

Father, let me not be as a talebearer who goes about revealing secrets, but let me be trustworthy and faithful in spirit. May my mind be as the mind of the wise, instructing my mouth, adding learning and persuasiveness to my lips I pray that I will speak pleasant words, which are sweetness to the soul and healing to the body. Lord, give me knowledge that I might spare my words, because even when a fool holds his peace he is considered wise. Help me to know when to close my lips so that I am esteemed a person of understanding. Guard my mouth and keep my soul from trouble. I will not associate with those who talk too freely; because for lack of wood, the fire goes out, and where there is no whisperer, contention ceases.

I will let another man praise me and not my own mouth; a stranger and not my own lips I will open my mouth with wisdom for in my tongue is the law of kindness.

Study: Col 4:6; 1 Pet 3:15; Prov 8:6-8; Prov 15:26; Prov 12:14; Prov 4:23,24; Prov 5:2; Prov 10:11; Eph 4:29; Prov 11:13; Prov 16: 23-24; Prov 3:8; Prov 17:28; Prov 21:23; Prov 26:20; Ps 27:2; Prov 31:26

Singles

Not one shall lack her mate. For My mouth has commanded it, and His Spirit has gathered them. Is 34:16

Father, I delight myself in You. Thank You for making me to ride on the high places of the earth, feeding me with the promises from Your Word. I seek out Your Word and read it, knowing that every word shall be fulfilled. No one shall lack his mate, for Your mouth has said it. I will not fear nor be ashamed during this time of singleness, for You, my Maker, are my Husband (spouse).

I believe that You have the perfect mate for me. I will not make haste but trust in You with all my heart, not leaning unto my own understanding. In all my ways I will acknowledge You and You will direct my paths. To everything there is a time and a season for every matter under heaven. I choose to be content while I wait for Your promise of a mate.

Thank You for a spirit of wisdom and revelation in the knowledge of You. The eyes of my understanding are being enlightened so that I may know what is the hope of Your calling and what are the riches of the glory of Your inheritance in the saints. Thank You that I am strengthened with might by Your

Spirit in the inner man and that I fulfill the plans and purposes You have for my life, in Jesus' Name.

Study: Is 58:14; Is 34:16; Is 54:4-5; Is 34:16; Prov 3:5-6; Ecc 3:1; Phil 4:11

Sexual Purity

Now the body is not for sexual immorality but for the Lord, and the Lord for the body. 1 Cor 6:13

Heavenly Father, I thank You for helping me to have sexual purity in my life. I present my body to You as a living sacrifice, holy, acceptable unto You, which is my reasonable service. I will not be conformed to this world, but rather transformed by the renewing of my mind, so that I may prove what is that good, acceptable and perfect will of God.

I hide Your Word in my heart so that I will not sin against You. Thank You for helping me to walk purely before You, not only spiritually, but physically. I abstain from all sexual activities other than within the confines of matrimony. I thank You that I am kept from adulterous acts, whether physical or mental. I do not covet or lust after another person's mate.

As Joseph fled from Potiphar's wife when she tried to seduce him, so I flee from all seducing spirits and individuals who seek my destruction. Thank You for helping me to possess my vessel in honor, to the glory of Your Name.

Study: Rom 12:1-2; Ps 119:11; 1 Pet 2:11; Gen 39:7-10; 1 Thes 4:4

For Men only.

I cleave to my own wife, cherishing and nourishing her as my own flesh, even as Christ does the church. I am one flesh with my wife and her body satisfies me at all times. I am always ravished with her love. None other can ever satisfy me, for You have provided me with the right mate and I thank You for her, in Jesus' Name.

Study: Gen 2:24; Eph 5:28-29; Prov 5:19

For Women only.

I cleave to my own husband, for we are one flesh. His heart can safely trust in me, for I will do him good and not evil all the days of my life. Our marriage is honorable in all and our bed undefiled. None other than my husband can satisfy me, for You have provided me with the right mate and I thank You for him, in Jesus' Name.

Study: Gen 2:24; Prov 31: 11-12; Heb 13:4

Chapter Three

PRAYERS FOR THE FAMILY

Father, pour upon this house the Spirit of grace and supplication. Fill all who dwell in this house with God's fullness and cause us to be rooted and grounded in love for one another. Lord, I believe You will do exceedingly above all I ask or think for this family. I pray that we would be drawn to one another as steel to a magnet and that grace, favor toward God and man be bestowed upon us.

Study: Eph 3:17-20

Wife's Prayer for Her Husband

The heart of her husband safely trusts her; So he will have no lack of gain. She does him good and not evil All the days of her life. Pro 31:11-12

Father, in the Name of Jesus, I pray and believe that my husband walks and lives, not in the counsel of the ungodly, following their advice, plans and purposes, nor does he sit in the seat of the scornful. But his delight is in the Word of God and in it he habitually meditates day and night. Therefore, he is like a tree that is planted and tended by the rivers of water, bringing forth fruit in its season. Thank You for granting him a spirit of wisdom and revelation, of insight into mysteries and secrets in the deep and intimate knowledge of You, so that his eyes are flooded with light, that he can know and understand the hope to which You have called him. Thank You Father, that my husband is a spiritual man and proves all things; yet he himself is judged by no one. He has the mind of Christ and understands the counsel and purposes of God.

Thank you that my husband is a doer of the Word and not merely a heedless hearer. By Your Spirit You implant and engrave Your laws in his heart and mind. Your Word shall not depart out of his mouth, nor out of the mouth of his children or grandchildren.

Study: Ps 1:1-3; Eph 1:17-18; 1 Cor 2:15-16; James 1:22; Jer 31:33; Is 59:21

Wife's Prayer for Herself

Do not let your adornment be merely outward – arranging the hair, wearing gold, or putting on fine apparel – rather let it be the hidden person of the heart, with the incorruptible beauty of a gentle and quiet spirit.
1 Pet 3:3-4

Father I thank You, in Jesus' Name that I am a capable, intelligent, patient, virtuous woman, and far more precious than jewels. My value to my husband and our family is far above rubies. His heart safely trusts in me. I will encourage, comfort and do them only good as long as there is life in me. I gird myself with strength, spiritual, mental and physical fitness for my God given task. I arise while it is night and get spiritual food for our household. I open my mouth with skillful and godly wisdom and on my tongue is the law of kindness and love. I look well to the way things go within our home and do not indulge in idleness, gossip, discontent or self pity. My husband and children rise up and call me blessed and happy. My husband boasts about and praises me.

I adapt myself to my husband and allow him to be the head of our home. My adorning is not merely outward, but it is rather the hidden person of the heart, with the incorruptible beauty of a gentle and quiet spirit, which is very precious in the sight of God. I am a good helpmate, suitable, adaptable, and I complete him. I am a crowning joy to him. I respect and reverence him, noticing, regarding, praising, loving and admiring him exceedingly. I am devoted to him and appreciate and prize him. We always think the best of each other and never return evil for evil or insult for insult, on the contrary, we return blessing for blessing.

Thank You Lord, for working in me both to will and to do of Your own good pleasure. I thank You that You help me to discern and know all things related to my husband and our family. I am sensitive to the Spirit of God. I have the mind of Christ. I have the thoughts and purposes of God for our family. I am a doer of God's Word and not a heedless hearer. Self-deception, pride, rebellion, fear, rejection, self-pity, envy and jealousy have no power over me. I cast down every imagination that exalts itself against the knowledge of God in my mind. I walk in the Spirit because I am full of the Spirit. I speak to myself in psalms, hymns and spiritual songs, making melody in my heart to the Lord at all times and in everything I give thanks. I walk in contentment and peace.

Study: Prov 31: 10-31; 1 Pet 3:3,4; Eph 5:33 (Amp); 1 Pet 3:9; 1 Cor 2:16;
James 1:22; 2 Cor 10:5; Gal 3:16; Col 3:16; Phil 4:11

Husband's Prayer for His Wife

She is your companion and your wife by covenant. But did He not make them one, having a remnant of the Spirit? Mal 2:14-15

Father I thank You, in Jesus' Name that my wife is a capable, intelligent, patient, virtuous woman and is far more precious than jewels. Her value to me and our family is far above rubies. My heart safely trusts in her. She will encourage, comfort and do us only good as long as there is life in her. She girds herself with strength, spiritual, mental and physical fitness for her God given task. She arises while it is night and gets spiritual food for our household. She opens her mouth with skillful and godly wisdom and on her tongue is the law of kindness and love. She looks well to the way things go within our home and does not indulge in idleness, gossip, discontent or self pity. Our children and I rise up and call her blessed and happy. I boast about her and praise her.

My wife adapts herself to me and allows me to be the head over our home. Her adorning is not merely outward, but it is rather the hidden person of the heart, with the incorruptible beauty of a gentle and quiet spirit, which is very precious in the sight of God. She is a good helpmate, suitable, adaptable, and she completes me. She is a crowning joy to me. She respects and reverences me, noticing, praising, loving and admiring me exceedingly. She is devoted to me and appreciates and prizes me. We always think the best of each other and never return evil for evil or insult for insult, but on the contrary, we return blessing for blessing.

Thank You Lord, for working in my wife both to will and to do of Your own good pleasure. I thank You that she discerns and knows all things related to me and our family and is sensitive to the Spirit of God. She has the mind of Christ. She has the thoughts, purposes and feelings of God for our family. She is a doer of God's Word and not a heedless hearer. Self-deception, pride, rebellion, fear, rejection, self-pity, envy and jealousy have no power over her. She casts down every imagination that exalts itself against the knowledge of God in her mind. She walks in the Spirit because she is full of the Spirit. She speaks to herself in psalms, hymns and spiritual songs, making melody in her heart to the Lord at all times and in everything gives thanks. Thank You for my wife, in Jesus' Name.

Study: Prov 31: 10-31; 1 Pet 3:3,4; Eph 5:33 (Amp); 1 Pet 3:9; Phil 2:13; 1 Cor 2:16; James 1:22; 2 Cor 10:5; Gal 5:16; Col 3:16

Husband's Prayer for Himself

Husbands, likewise, dwell with them with understanding, giving honor to the wife, as to the weaker vessel, and as being heirs together of the grace of life, that your prayers may not be hindered. 1 Pet 37

Father, in the Name of Jesus, I pray and believe that I walk and live, not in the counsel of the ungodly, following their advice, plans and purposes, nor do I sit in the seat of the scornful. My delight is in the Word of God, wherein I habitually meditate day and night. Therefore, I am like a tree that is planted and tended by the rivers of water, bringing forth fruit in its season. Thank You for granting me a spirit of wisdom and revelation, of insight into mysteries and secrets in the deep and intimate knowledge of You, so that my eyes are flooded with light, that I can know and understand the hope to which You have called me and my family. Thank You Father, in Jesus' Name that I am a spiritual man and try all things; yet I myself am judged by no one. I have the mind of Christ and understand the counsels and purposes of God and hold the thoughts and purposes of God's heart.

Thank You for helping me to be a doer of the Word and not merely a heedless hearer. By Your Spirit You implant and engrave Your laws in my heart and mind. Your Word shall not depart out of my mouth, nor out of the mouth of my children or grandchildren.

Study: Ps 1:1-3; Eph 1:17; 1 Cor 2:15-16; James 1:22; Jer 31:33

Protection of Marriage

Your wife shall be like a fruitful vine In the very heart of your house, Your children like olive plants All around your table. Ps 128:3

Thank You, Father, that in Jesus' Name my husband is the head of our home, even as Christ is the head of the Church. He is considerate and thoughtful of my needs and dwells with me according to spiritual understanding. Knowing that we are heirs together of the grace of God, our prayers are not hindered because we walk in love and unity, preferring and favoring one another. One shall chase a thousand, but my husband and I shall put ten thousand to flight. A three-fold cord is not easily broken. When we agree together as touching anything that we shall ask, it shall be done for us by You, Father.

Thank You Lord, that our fountain of human life is blessed with the rewards of fidelity and my husband rejoices with me, the wife of his youth. I thank You that my bosom satisfies him at all times and he is always transported with delight in my love.

The heart of my husband safely trusts in me and senses my support and affection. He will never be infatuated with a loose woman or embrace the bosom of an outsider and go astray. Discretion and understanding watch over him and keep and deliver him from the alien and evil woman and from the outsider with her flattering words. He does not lust after her beauty or bosom.

I remind you Satan, that no weapon formed against my husband or our marriage shall prosper, in Jesus' Name. I command every manipulative, controlling, seducing spirit of lust to flee from him in seven ways. Every lying spirit of division, separation and divorce is powerless against us in the Name of Jesus. Every oppressor or weapon formed against us and our marriage will be destroyed in mutually destructive wars. Our marriage is blessed and what God has joined together no man shall put asunder. We are joint heirs with Jesus of the grace of God and we live and move in unity. God has commanded His blessings on us because we work and live together in harmony.

Thank You Father, that you give us wisdom, knowledge and discernment in rearing our children tenderly by the training, discipline, counsel and admonition of the Lord. We will not irritate or provoke our children to anger nor exasperate them. We will not indulge our anger or resentment on our children by undue chastisement nor set ourselves to their ruin. We will not be hard on our children, nor harass them, lest they become discouraged, sullen and morose and feel inferior and frustrated. We will not break their spirit. Thank You for helping us to teach and command our children to keep the ways of the Lord and to do what is just and righteous. Thank You Father, that You have turned the heart of my husband to our children and their hearts to him.

Even if my husband does not obey the Word of God he will be won by my godly life and the inward adorning of a gentle and peaceful spirit.

Study: Eph 5:23-28; 1 Pet 3:7; Lev 26:8; Ecc 4:12; Matt 18:19; Prov 5:18; Prov 5:24; Prov 31:11; Prov 2:11,16; Is 54:17; Matt 19:6; 1 Pet 3:7; Ps 133:1; Eph 6:4; Col 3:21; Mal. 4;6; 1 Pet 3:1

Protection and Guidance

In all your ways acknowledge Him, And He shall direct your paths. Pro 3:6

Satan, I bind your powers over my mind in Jesus' Name. I command every imagination that exalts itself against the knowledge of God to be cast down from my mind. I take every thought captive and make them submissive to the obedience of Christ. I render every former tyrant master powerless and dead over my mind. They shall not reappear, they are powerless ghosts. Every reasoning, intellectual, self-sufficient, independent, humanistic, spirit of pride, every spirit of rejection and fear of man is rendered powerless against me in the Name of Jesus. Thank You Lord, that every stubborn wall of resistance in me is crushed by the hammer of Your Word. I trust in You with all my heart and do not lean unto my own understanding. In all my ways I will acknowledge You and You will direct and make straight and plain my paths.

I hearken diligently to Your commands, and Your blessings overtake me. I am blessed coming in and blessed going out. I am the head and not the tail; I am above only and not beneath. When the enemy comes against me one way, he flees before me seven ways. Thank You Father, that I am a diligent, hard worker and provide for my family. I am known in the city gates and have favor, high esteem and good understanding with God and man.

Study: 2 Cor 10:5; Is 26: 12-14; Jer 23:29; Prov 3:5,6; Deut 28:1-7; Prov 22:29; Prov 31:23

Psalm 91—Family Protection

My family and I dwell in the secret place of the Most High. We abide under the shadow of the Almighty, whose power no foe can withstand. We say of the Lord, "He is my Refuge and my Fortress, my God in whom I trust." He surely delivers us from every trap of the enemy so that our feet are not caught in a hidden snare or danger. A thousand may fall at our side and ten thousand at our right hand, but it shall not come near us. Only spectators shall we be as we witness the reward of the wicked.

Because we have made the Lord our refuge and the Most High our dwelling place, there shall no evil befall us, nor any plague or calamity come near us. For the Lord has given His angels charge over us to accompany, defend and preserve us in all of our ways of service and obedience. We have set our love upon You O Lord, therefore You deliver us and set us on high. When we call upon You, You will answer. You will be with us in trouble. You will deliver and honor us. With long life You will satisfy us and show us Your salvation.

Health and Healing for the Family

So you shall serve the LORD your God, and He will bless your bread and your water. And I will take sickness away from the midst of you. Ex 23:25

Father, I thank You that Jesus came to bring us life and life more abundantly. Jesus Himself bore all sickness, disease and infirmity. Cancer, viruses, heart disease, infectious and contaminating diseases, AIDS, the infirmities of age and even death itself He bore in His own body on the tree. Therefore, death and sickness have no power over my family and me, for by His stripes we were healed.

We are redeemed from the curse of the law. Every sickness and disease is under the curse of the law, therefore we are redeemed from them all. Sin and death have no dominion over us. We are alive unto righteousness and health. Those sins and diseases from our forefathers have no supremacy or dominion over us because the blood of Jesus stripped them of their power and made a show of them openly, triumphing over them. The blood of Jesus has obtained an everlasting redemption and release for us by destroying these curses in Jesus' Name.

You bless our bread and our water as we serve You, therefore sickness has been taken from our midst and the number of our days we will fulfill. Our bodies are the temple of the Holy Ghost. The Spirit of the living God dwells in us. We are not our own but we are bought with a price. The very presence of the Living God within us preserves us from the evil of sin, sickness, and disease (name it). Therefore Satan, take your hands off of God's temple. Our bodies glorify God by being in divine health so that we can serve our God with our whole heart, soul and body. We are delivered from the power of darkness. The law of the Spirit of life in Christ Jesus has made us free from all the law of sin and death.

We have no fear because Jesus brought to nought the devil, who had the power of death. Satan, Jesus destroyed your power. Therefore, loose our bodies from all sickness (be specific). Body (name parts), come into line with the Word of God. Sickness (name it), bow to the Name of Jesus. The Name of Jesus is above your name. Old things are passed away and all things have been made new. Greater is He that is in us than he that is in the world. Thank You, for divine health, in Jesus' Name.

Study: John 10:10; Matt 8:17; 1 Pet. 2:24; Gal 3:13; Deut 28:61; Col 2:15; Heb 9:12; Ex 23:25; 1 Cor 6:19; Col 1:13; Rom 8:2; Heb 2:14; Phil 2:10; 2 Cor 5:17; 1 John 4:4

Finances

The young lions lack and suffer hunger; But those who seek the Lord shall not lack any good thing. Ps 34:10

Father, in Jesus' Name, I declare that my family does not rob God by withholding our tithes and offerings. We are tithers, faithfully bringing all our tithes, the whole tenth of our income, into our local church, that there may be food in Your house. Because we have given, You have promised that the windows of heaven are opened to us and the blessings being poured out are so abundant that there is not room enough to receive them all. I thank You for rebuking the devourer for our sakes. He shall not destroy the fruit of our ground, or steal our source of income.

The Lord is a refuge and a high tower for us, and a stronghold in times of trouble (high costs, destitution and desperation). Thank You Father, in Jesus' Name, for laying up the wealth of the sinner to place into the hands of the just.

Thank You that You supply all of our needs according to Your riches in glory by Christ Jesus. Thank You Lord, that You are able and are making all grace, every favor and earthly blessing come to us in abundance, so that we always, under all circumstances, and whatever the need, are self sufficient, possessing enough to require no aid or support, and furnished in abundance for every good work and charitable donation.

We give and gifts are given to us, good measure, pressed down, shaken together and running over will they pour into my family's bosom. Thank You Lord, that You bring a hundred fold return to us in response to our giving.

In Jesus' Name, I rebuke the devourer from our finances, jobs, our home and our possessions. I command you Satan to take your hands off our money and property. We are not under the curse of poverty. We are redeemed from it! So, we resist you and you must flee from our finances, in Jesus' Name.

Study: Mal 3:8-12; Ps 59:16; Prov 13:22; Phil 4:19; 2 Cor 9:8; Luke 6:38; Mal 3:11; James 4:7

Chapter Four

PRAYERS FOR CHILDREN

Prayer For Conception

*By faith Sarah herself also received strength to conceive seed, and she
bore a child when she was past the age, because she judged Him
faithful who had promised.* Heb 11:11

Father God I come before You knowing that barrenness is a
curse and we as believers are redeemed from the curse.
Therefore I call Heaven and Earth to witness that I choose life
that both my seed and I shall live.

I thank You Father God that my body is wonderfully and
perfectly created by the hand of God. It is a God design and it
will function as it was created to function. I speak to my
ovaries and uterus to fulfill their God directed purpose and be
healthy and normal in Jesus' Name! I believe and confess with
my mouth that my body is a sanctuary for the Holy Spirit and
the very life force of God dwells within me. I have this
confidence in God that what I ask is the will and purpose of
God and He hears me and will give me the desire of my heart.

My husband and I stand in agreement with the Word of God
that we are a blessed people and shall not be barren. No evil
can overcome us or plague come upon our home. For we have
made the Lord God our refuge and in His blessing we
continually dwell.

You said that You are our God and we are Your people. You
will bless us and multiply us and bless the fruit of my womb.
We declare by faith that neither male nor female among Your
people shall be barren.

Study: Gal 3:13; Deut 30:19, Ps 139:14; Rom 10:10; 1 John 5:14-15; Deut 7:14; Ps 91:9-10; Deut 7:13

Prayer For Pregnancy

Blessed are you among women, and blessed is the fruit of your womb!
Luke 1:27

I thank You and praise You Father God for the precious gift of my child. This child has been chosen by God and is being knit together in my womb. I can rejoice with the words of Hannah, for this child I prayed and the Lord has given me the petition I asked of him.

I rebuke the thief who comes to kill, steal and destroy, for my child is a gift from God. Miscarriage, premature delivery, and the curse of death is broken over my body. I am confident that He who began a good work in me will fulfill it. I am a fruitful vine in my home and my children will be like healthy olive plants around my table.

Blessing and life are in my words, so I speak to my body and my baby to be in perfect health and strength. My child will develop as You ordered it to. I declare its skeleton, brains, spinal cord, vital organs and every cell, tissue and inward part of its body will develop as God has ordered.

I also speak to my uterus, amniotic fluid, umbilical cord and every related part of my body, that this is its God appointed time and every necessary part will function as has God directed.

I am a born again believer and the very life of Christ dwells in me. Therefore, I have soundness of spirit, soul and body. I am emotionally, physically and spiritually prepared for a healthy, successful pregnancy. To everything there is a time and season and my body's purpose at this time is to conceive, carry my baby and to give birth at the appointed day.

Study: 1 Sam 1:2-7; Ex 23:26; Phil 1:6; Ps 128:3; Ecc 1:1-2

Prayer For Supernatural Childbirth

She will be saved in childbearing if they continue in faith, love, and holiness, with self-control. 1 Tim 2:15

Thank You Father God for my precious healthy baby and a strong able body. On a God-appointed day my body will give birth just as it was created by God to do. Every organ, tissue, ligament and muscle will fulfill their designed purpose to deliver my baby without undue pain or complications.

My child was knit together in my womb by the hand of God and will be born normal and healthy. My God has not given me a spirit of fear, but I have a spirit of power, love, and a focused, well balanced mind. I seek the Lord and He hears me and I am delivered from all my fears.

I cast down any imagination or fear from my own or other women's previous experiences that come against the Word of God. I bring any thoughts that would bring fear, captive to the word of God. I know the thoughts God has toward my child and I, thoughts of peace and not evil, to give me the expected end.

God's purpose is for us to go forth and multiply. Marriage and children are the plan and blessing of God. I can see and believe that my children are a blessing of God. I can see and believe that my children are a heritage of the Lord, and the fruit of the womb is His reward. Let all this be according to my faith, for whatever I believe I shall have.

Study: 2 Tim 1:7; Ps 34:4; 2 Cor 10:5; Jer 29:11; Gen 1:22

Prayer For Post-Partum Depression

As soon as she has given birth to the child, she no longer remembers the anguish, for joy that a human being has been born into the world.
John 16:21

I thank You O God that I am blessed and Your promise to me is I shall be the keeper of my home and a joyful mother of children. Therefore, I stand at the door of my home and declare that no evil shall befall me, and no plague shall come near my dwelling.

I speak with the authority of the believer, that Christ has born my griefs and carried my sorrows. He was wounded for my transgressions and the chastisement of my peace was upon Him, and by His stripes I am physically, emotionally and mentally healed.

All my needs are abundantly supplied by His riches and anything I lack my God has provided for me. Knowing this I speak to every chemical and mental need and draw on my creators supply. Anything I lack mentally, spiritually or physically is met with His abundance. I also speak to my hormones that they are balanced and perfectly adjusted and that my emotions, perceptions and reactions are calm and balanced.

I seek the Lord and He hears me and delivers me from all my fears. When I lay down I will not be afraid for my child, myself or my family. I shall lay down and experience sweet sleep. Faith comes by hearing, and hearing by the Word of God. Therefore, I diligently seek the Lord, He is my peace and very present help in time of need. I overcome by the Word of God and the power of my testimony.

Study: Ps 113:9; Ps 9:10; Isa 53:4-5; Phil 4:19; Ps 34:4; Rom 10:17

Praying Over Your Children

Blessed is the man who fears the LORD, who delights greatly in His commandments. His descendants will be mighty on earth; the generation of the upright will be blessed. Ps 112:1-2

Father, in the Name of Jesus, I believe that because my children are brought up in the way that they should go, they shall not depart from Your Word when they are old. Thank You that my children attend to Your Word. They do not let it depart from their sight, but keep it in the centre of their hearts and it is life to them, healing and health to all their flesh. Thank You that my children guard and keep their hearts with all diligence for out of their hearts flow the springs of life. I pray that my children would put away from themselves false and dishonest speech, willful and contrary talk. Place a guard on their lips so that no corrupt communication shall proceed out of their mouths but only that which is to the use of edifying that it may minister grace to the hearers. I pray that my children will set their affections always on Jesus and the things above and not on the things of this earth. Their ways will be established and ordered aright and their feet shall be kept from evil.

Thank You Father, in Jesus' Name that Your Word will lead my children. When they sleep, it shall keep them. When they awaken, it shall talk to them. Your Word is a lamp unto their feet and a light unto their path. Thank You Lord, that by Your Spirit You imprint and engrave Your laws upon their minds and hearts and Your Word shall not depart out of their mouths nor out of the mouths of their children or grandchildren.

I pray that my children will delight greatly in Your commandments. Thank You for imparting the fear of the Lord to my children so they will hate evil and love righteousness. Thank You for causing my children to increase in wisdom, stature and favor with God and man. They shall be mighty upon the earth.

Thank You Lord, that we would be visionary parents to draw out the gifts and talents of our children in Jesus' Name.

Study: Prov 4:20-23; Ps 141:3; Eph 4:29; Col 3:2; Prov 6:20-24; Ps 119:105; Jer 31:33; Ps 112:1-2; Luke 2:40

Guidance for Children

Hear, my son, and receive my sayings, and the years of your life will be many. Prov 4:10

I confess that my children do not walk after the counsel of the ungodly, nor do they stand in the way of sinners, or sit in the seat of the scornful, but their delight is in Your Word. In it they meditate day and night. To them all things are pure, for they are pure.

My children walk in the way of good men and women and keep to the path of the consistently righteous. In Jesus' Name, I command every evil, alien, adulterous man, woman or child to be removed from their path. Every seductive, manipulative, rebellious and controlling spirit of lust is bound and rendered useless, powerless and ineffective against them. They are not taken by any alien person's beauty or flattering speech, for discretion watches over my children and understanding keeps them.

I pray that my children will always hear the voice of the Good Shepherd and that they will be filled with the knowledge of Your will in all wisdom and spiritual understanding so that they may know the hope of Your calling and the glorious inheritance they have as saints in light, and the exceeding greatness of You power towards them. I pray that they will live a life that is worthy of You and pleases You, bearing fruit in every good work, growing in the knowledge of God, being strengthened with all might according to Your glorious power so that they exercise every kind of endurance and patience with joy.

I believe You guide my children with Your eye, Father, and teach them in the way they should go. Thank You that they walk in the light as You are in the light, and that they have fellowship with one another and the blood of Jesus cleanses them from all sin. Thank You for making their pathway brighter and clearer every day.

Study: Ps 1:1-2; Titus 1:5; John 10:4-5; Col 1:9; Eph 1:18-19; Col 1:10-11; Ps 32:8; 1 John 1:7; Prov 4:18

Children Knowing God's Love

Train up a child in the way he should go, And when he is old he will not depart from it. Prov 22:6

I pray that their love may abound yet more and more and extend to its fullest development. In knowledge and in all insight, may they have a comprehensive discernment to prove what is vital and of real value. I pray that they may be untainted, pure, unerring and blameless until the day of Christ and be filled with the fruits of righteousness which come through Jesus Christ, to the glory of God.

I believe that You strengthen my children according to the riches of Your glory with might by Your Spirit in the inner man; that Christ may dwell in their hearts by faith, that they will be rooted and grounded in love and be able to comprehend with all the saints what is the breadth, length, depth and height of Your love. I thank You that they know the love of Christ, which passes knowledge, that they may be filled with all the fullness of God.

Study: Phil 1:9; Phil 1:11; Eph 3:18-20

Protection for Children

*Take heed that you do not despise one of these little ones, for I say to you that
in heaven their angels always see the face of My Father who is in heaven.*
Matt 18:10

Father, I thank You that my children delight to do Your will and
that they obey and honor their parents, for this is right and well-
pleasing to You. Therefore You have promised that all will go
well with them and they will live long on the earth. Thank You
that no evil shall befall them, nor shall any plague or calamity
come nigh our dwelling, for You give Your angels charge over us
to keep us in all our ways. I bind and take authority over every
rebellious spirit, every controlling, manipulative, lying spirit,
every spirit of fear and rejection, and all spirits of strife and I
command you all to be far removed from my home and children,
in Jesus' Name! I speak confusion to every oppressor over my
children and command them to be destroyed in mutually
destructive wars. No weapon formed against my children shall
prosper and every tongue that rises in judgment against them
shall be shown to be in the wrong. This peace, righteousness and
security that triumphs over opposition is the heritage of the
servants of the Lord.

Thank You for the abundance of grace that delivers my children
from all sin and teaches them to reject all ungodliness, worldly
passions and lusts. I thank You that they live discreet, temperate,
self-controlled, upright, devout and spiritually whole lives in this
present world. My children present their bodies a living sacrifice
unto You, and are not conformed to this world, but they are
transformed by the renewing of their minds so that they prove
the good, acceptable and perfect will of God in their lives.

I pray in Jesus' Name that my children will abstain from evil,
shrink from it and keep aloof from it. I also pray that the God of

peace Himself will sanctify them through and through and separate them from profane things, making them pure and wholly consecrated to You Lord, so that their spirit, soul and body will be preserved blameless at the coming of our Lord Jesus Christ.

All my children are taught of the Lord and great is their peace and undisturbed composure. Thank You that when they lie down they shall not be afraid, but their sleep shall be sweet for they have not been given a spirit of fear, but of power, of love and a sound mind.

I break the power of every spirit of witchcraft and every harassing, tormenting spirit of fear over my children. I command these forces to be destroyed in mutually destructive wars. Your pavilion of peace covers my children at all times. Every former tyrant master is dead and shall not come back to my children because the blood of Jesus has stripped them of their power. These curses from the forefathers have no supremacy over my children because they are covered with the blood of Jesus which has delivered them from the powers of darkness and translated them into the kingdom of Your dear Son.

Study: Ps 40:8; Eph 6:1-3; Ps 9:10-11; Is 54:17; Titus 2:12; Rom 12:1-2; 1 Thes 5:23; Is 54:13; Prov 3:24; 2 Tim 1:7; Is 26:12-14

Prayer for Learning

I have more understanding than all my teachers, For Your testimonies are my meditation. Ps 119:99

Father, I thank You that my children have the mind of Christ. They are without blemish, well-favored in appearance, skillful in all wisdom, discernment and understanding, apt in learning and knowledge and competent to complete every new learning experience.

Thank You Holy Spirit, that You lead and guide them and help them to learn and give them supernatural recall of what they have studied. Thank You that they have clear, sound, agile, and alert minds and can do all things through Christ who strengthens them.

Thank You Father, that Your Word makes my children wiser than their enemies, teachers and those who are older and more experienced than they are. Thank You that their teachers and instructors are not able to resist the intelligence and inspiration of the Spirit with which they speak or write when doing their assigned tasks.

Thank You Lord, for delivering them with knowledge and superior discernment so that they are alert to hidden snares and traps. Thank You that they walk in the light as You are in the light and the blood of Jesus cleanses them from all sin. Thank You that their pathway becomes brighter and brighter even as the dawn of a new day.

Therefore, I bind all dullness, tiredness, forget-fulness, disorganization, slumber, apathy, heaviness, discouragement, confusion and every power of darkness assigned to my children, in Jesus' Name. I command these forces to be loosed from their minds. Their minds are submitted to God and controlled by the Holy Spirit. I command their minds to concentrate and come into line with the Word of God. Thank You for the victory, in Jesus' Name!

Study: I Cor 2:16; Dan 1:4; Phil 4:13; Ps 119: 98-100; 1 John 1:7; Prov 4:18;

Purity for Teenagers

*How can a young man cleanse his way? By taking heed according
to Your word.* Ps 119:9

I thank You Father, in Jesus' Name, that my children keep their
way pure by taking heed to and living according to Your Word.
No one looks down on them, even though they are young, for
they set an example for the believers, in conduct, speech, in life,
in love, in spirit, in faith and in purity. They flee youthful lusts
and pursue righteousness, faith, love and peace with all those
who call on the Lord out of a pure heart. They present their
bodies as living sacrifices, holy and acceptable unto You, which is
their reasonable service. They are not conformed to this world,
but are transformed by the constant renewing of their minds, so
they may prove what is that good, acceptable and perfect will of
God. They do not present the members of their bodies as
instruments of unrighteousness to sin, but present themselves to
God, as those who are alive from the dead, and their members as
instruments and weapons of righteousness. Sin shall not have
dominion over them.

To my children are all things pure, for they are pure. My children
keep their father's command and do not forsake the law of their
mother. They bind them continually upon their hearts and tie
them around their necks. When they roam, Your Word leads
them, when they sleep, it keeps them, and when they awake it
speaks with them. For Your commandment is a lamp to them
and Your law is their light. The reproof of Your instruction is
their way of life. They keep them from the evil woman, from the
flattering tongue of a seductress. They do not lust after her
beauty in their hearts, nor do they let her allure them with her
eyelids.

Thank You that You are able and will keep my children from
falling, and will present them before the presence of Your glory

with exceeding joy. Unto You be glory and majesty, dominion and power, both now and forever, in Jesus' Name!

Study: Ps 119:9; 1 Tim 4:12; 2 Tim 2:22; Rom 12:1; Rom 6:13,14; Titus 1:5; Prov 6: 22-24; Jude 24

Protection from Wrong Mate

Reproofs of instruction are the way of life, to keep you from the evil woman, from the flattering tongue of a seductress. Prov 6:23-24

Thank You Lord, that my children have the mind of Christ. They examine, prove, investigate and discern all things. Thank You for delivering them from every strange, alien, evil, conniving person, in Jesus' Name. They do not lust after their beauty and are not taken by the flattery of their liPs Understanding and discretion watch over them and they are delivered through knowledge and superior discernment.

In Jesus' Name, I break the power of all manipulation, control, witchcraft, lust, darkness, lying and seducing spirits over my children. I speak confusion into every hidden snare and trap of Satan and I command them to be destroyed in mutually destructive wars. I command every deceitful worker to be removed from their paths, in Jesus' Name. Thank You Father, for the angels that surround and encamp about my children, so that they are kept in all of their ways. You are leading them to the right mate and they will find them.

Study: 1 Cor 2:16; Prov 2:11; Ps 91:11

Right Wife for Son

Who can find a virtuous wife? For her worth is far above rubies. Prov 31:10

Father, I thank You for the right helpmate for my son, one who will aid, surround, assist and complete him. Thank You that she will joyfully submit herself to him as the head of their home and to the call of God on his life and be a crowning joy to him. She will do him only good and not evil all the days of her life.

Thank You, in Jesus' Name, for that virtuous woman who is intelligent, strong in the Lord, courageous and war-like; who will be a woman of the Word. I pray for one who will walk in the spirit and not fulfill the lusts of the flesh, one that causes her husband to be known in the city gates. Strength and honor are her clothing. Thank You for a mate who has discretion, who opens her mouth with wisdom and on her tongue is the law of kindness. She does not indulge in idleness, self-pity, gossip or malcontent, but fears the Lord. Thank You Lord, that she is a doer of the Word and not a heedless hearer. She will look well to the ways of her household and will be as an intercessor for her husband and children.

I thank You for that virtuous woman for my son who is rooted and grounded in love and not in envy, jealousy and selfish ambition. She seeks the kingdom of God first and will not be as Lot's wife looking to the pleasures of this life, but will lose her life so that she, her husband and children can gain the higher life. I pray for one whose affections are on things above and not on the things below.

Study: Gen 2:18; Prov 12:4; Prov 31:12; Gal 5:16; James 1:22; Eph 3:17; Matt 6:33; Col 3:2

Harmony in Son's Marriage

Her children rise up and call her blessed; Her husband also, and he praises her. Prov 31:28

Thank You also, Father, that my son will love his wife as Christ loves the church. He will nourish and cherish and protect her. He will rise up and call her blessed, and boast about and praise her. He will dwell with her with supernatural understanding and give honor and compliments abundantly unto her, as being heirs together of the grace of God, so their prayers are not hindered. They will be of one mind, having compassion for one another, loving, tender and courteous to one another, not returning evil for evil or reviling for reviling, but rather blessing, knowing that they were called to this, that they may inherit a blessing.

Thank You that the fountain of their human life is blessed with the rewards of fidelity. My son will rejoice with the wife of his youth. She will be loving and pleasant; her body will satisfy him at all times, and he will be always ravished with her love.

Study: Eph 5:25-29; Prov 31:28; 1 Pet 3:7-9; Prov 5: 18-19

Right Husband for Daughter

So husbands ought to love their own wives as their own bodies; he who loves his wife loves himself. Eph 5:28

Father in Jesus' Name, I thank You for a mate for my daughter who seeks Your Kingdom and Your righteousness first. He shall be one who will set his mind and affection on the things which are above and not on the things which are below.

Thank You Father, that skillful and godly wisdom has entered into his heart and knowledge is pleasant to him. He is a man who puts his trust in You and leans not unto his own understanding.

You are his confidence. You keep his foot from being caught in a trap or hidden danger.

Thank You Father, that my daughter's husband is a mighty man of faith and valor who walks by faith and not by sight. He knows his God and shall be strong and do exploits in Jesus' Name. Thank You for that one who possesses an excellent spirit, who speaks excellent and princely things, holding to the professing of his faith without wavering. He is as bold as a lion.

Thank You Lord, that he guards his heart with all vigilance and puts away from him all false and dishonest speech, willful and contrary talk. Thank You for a mate who hearkens diligently to Your Word, is a doer of it and not a heedless hearer. He is not tossed to and fro by every wind of doctrine, but rather always walking in truth. In his pathway is life and not death.

Thank You Lord, for a diligent, hard worker who is not a sluggard, but provides for the needs of his own household. He bears himself becomingly, is correct and honorable and commands the respect of the outside world by being self-supporting and hard working.

Father, I thank You for that mate who will be the head of his home. He will love my daughter as his own body, will nourish and cherish her. He will be satisfied with the wife of his youth and not embrace the bosom of an outsider. Thank You that he guards over his spirit so that it is controlled by Your Spirit. He walks in the Spirit and does not fulfill the lusts of the flesh. He has the mind of Christ, discerns, examines, proves and knows all things.

Thank You that my daughter's mate does not faint in the day of adversity, but is strong in the Lord and in the power of His might. He is rooted and grounded in love. Thank You that he will command his children as Abraham did, bringing them up tenderly in the nurture and admonition of the Lord and will not provoke them to wrath.

Study: Matt 6:33; Col 3:2; Prov 2:10; Prov 3:5; 2 Cor 5:7; Dan 11:32; Prov 4:23; James 1:22; Eph 4:14; Prov 12:28; Prov 22:29; Eph 5:29; Prov 5:19; Gal 5:6; 1 Cor 2:16; Prov 24:10; Eph 6:10; Eph 3:17; Eph 6:4

Daughter's Role in Marriage

Wives, submit to your own husbands, as to the Lord. Eph 5:22

I thank You that my daughter does not lust after any alien man. In the Name of Jesus, I break the power of every seductive, manipulative, controlling spirit of lust over her. I command these seducing spirits to be powerless, useless and ineffective against her. She will not be drawn into a wrong relationship.

Thank You that my daughter will submit herself to her own husband as unto the Lord; that his heart will safely trust in her because she will do him good and not evil all the days of her life. Help her, Father, to speak words of wisdom and may kindness be the rule for all she says. Thank You for giving her the ornament of a gentle and quiet spirit. Thank You that she will respect and honor her husband and be a crowning joy to him. He will rejoice with the wife of his youth, for she is loving and pleasant. Her body will satisfy him at all times and he will always be ravished with her love.

Thank You for that mighty man of faith and valor for my daughter. Thank You that he will come at the right time for my daughter. In Jesus' Name.

Study: Eph 5:22; Prov 31:12; 1 Pet 3:4; Eph 5:33; Prov 5: 18-19

You Are My God

Encounter the intimacy and glory of God through His Names

You Are....

My Abba Father, my Papa God   Rom 8:15

All- sufficient, my all-sufficiency (El Shaddai)   2 Cor 12:9-10

My Answer   Ps 20:6

My Banner of victory   Zeph 2:16

My Burden-bearer   Ps 68:19

My Cornerstone, My sure foundation   Is 28:16

My Unshakable Confidence   Prov3:26

My Covenant-keeping God   Deut 7:9

My Desire, more precious than silver   Prov 3:13-15

My Glory, the lifter of my head   Ps 3:3

Ever-present, always with me, available, near   Matt 1:23

My Joy and song   John 15:11

My Hiding place   Ps 32:7

My very present help in time of need   Ps 46:1

The God of miracles who works wonders for me   Ps 72:18

My God who is always there   Rev 21:7

My Lamp, my light   Ps 27:1

My Living bread, living water   John 7:37-38

Love, loving, lover of my soul   Rom 8:35-39

Chapter Five

PRAYERS FOR PERSONAL GROWTH

Confessing Who I Am In Christ

I thank You Father that I am a new creation. The old things have passed away and all things have become new. I am part of a chosen generation, a royal priesthood, and a holy nation. I will proclaim Your praises, for You have called me out of darkness and into Your marvelous light.

I am Your workmanship, created in Christ Jesus for good works, which You have prepared beforehand for me to walk in. I thank You that there is therefore now no condemnation to those who are in Christ Jesus, who do not walk according to the flesh, but according to the Spirit. I am a child of God because I believe in Your Name. Therefore I have been received by Christ, and He has adopted me, which is His good pleasure.

I am the righteousness of God! I am a temple of the Holy Spirit and He dwells in me. I will not be conformed to this world, but be transformed by the renewing of my mind, so that I may prove what is that good and acceptable and perfect will of God for my life.

I am an overcomer, because greater is He that is in me than he who is in the world. I have life through the Son, for the Word says that "He who has the Son has life". I am born of God, and the wicked one, the devil, cannot touch me. In the world there may be tribulation, but I can be of good cheer for You have overcome the world and therefore, I can do all things through Christ who strengthens me!

Study: 2 Cor 5:17; 1 Pet 2:9; Eph 2:10; Rom 8:1; John 1:12; Eph 1:5; 1 Cor 6:19; Rom 12:2; 1 John 4:4; 1 Cor 12:27; John 15:15; 1 John 5:12, 18; John 16:33; Phil 4:13

Consecration and Dedication

He died for all, that those who live should live no longer for themselves, but for Him who died for them and rose again. 2 Cor 5:15

I dedicate myself to You, precious Father. I pray that love be perfected in me. Because I am born of God, I know that the love which springs from You also dwells in me. I desire that I decrease and that You increase and grow more prominent in me. I lay myself upon Your altar today, desirous of this: that I may consecrate myself wholly unto You, that Your perfect will, not mine, be accomplished in me. Cleanse me, O Father, from all known and unknown sin and sanctify me wholly unto You.

Father God, today I dedicate my body unto You. I present all my members and faculties as living sacrifices; holy, devoted, consecrated and well pleasing to You as spiritual worship. I will not be conformed to this world or this age, which is fashioned after and adapted to its external, superficial customs, but I will be transformed and changed by the entire renewal of my mind, by its new ideals and attitudes, so that I may prove what is Your good and acceptable and perfect will.

I shall be sanctified and cleansed with the washing of water by Your Word, O Lord. Let Your will be done in my life and not my own. Lord, You are my Father; I am the clay in Your hands and You are the potter. I am the work of Your hands. Mold me Lord, and make me into what seems good to You, a vessel fit for Your use. In Jesus' Name.

Study: 1 John 4:7; John 3:30; Rom 12:1-2; Eph 5:26; Is 64:8;

Prayer For Destiny

For I know the thoughts that I think toward you, says the LORD,
thoughts of peace and not of evil, to give you a future and a hope.
Jer 29:11

I come to You Lord in the Mighty Name of Jesus. I know You are all powerful, all knowing and all consuming. I thank You that You have a plan and a purpose for my life. I look to You to guide and direct me in the way I am to go.

I decree that the plan of the Lord for my life will come forth and that You will reveal that plan step by step in Your perfect timing. I trust in You Lord that You will not lead me to calamity but that You give me a future and a hope. I will wait upon Your timing Lord for I know You have an appointed time. Even when it seems that things are taking a long time, I will trust You with my future.

I declare that You will accomplish all that concerns me. You are loving and kind and would never forsake me. Open my eyes and ears that I may perceive Your ways and directions daily. I call forth my destiny in Jesus' Name. Lord, I will sow good things along my pathway so I can reap good results. I will endeavour to walk with You in an attitude of gratitude and obedience to Your Word and Your voice. I know You are a rewarder of those who diligently seek You. I ask for You to open the doors that need to be opened before me. I ask You to bring to my life the people who will instruct, correct and watch over me.

Everything You have spoken through Your leaders into my life and about my future WILL be accomplished and will not return void. You are the God of the impossible and I thank You that You will make all things possible in my life.

Lord, I surrender my fears of man and of the future and I put my trust in you. You used Moses in a mighty way even though he could not speak. Lord, I commit myself to You today. Have Your way in my life and use me for the furtherance of Your kingdom. I lay down my plans and my desires and choose Your destiny for my life.

Guide me daily! Make my way plain so I may follow Your voice. Bring those to me that I may encourage, teach, deliver or heal.

I thank You that You cause all things to work together for good to those who love God, to those who are called according to His purpose. I love You Lord and I believe that I am Your child and full of purpose.

I thank You that as I step out with You, Your light and Your love will shine through me and that my destiny will unfold before me. I now commit my works and plans to You Lord that Your plans will be established in my life. In Jesus' Name I pray. Amen

Study: Jer 29:11-13; Hab 2:3; Ps 138:8; Gal 6:7; Heb 11:6; Is 55:11; Rom 8:28; Prov 16:3

Favor

Let not mercy and truth forsake you; bind them around your neck, write them on the tablet of your heart, and so find favor and high esteem in the sight of God and man. Prov 3:3-4

Father, I will not let mercy, kindness and truth forsake me but will bind them about my neck and write them upon the tablets of my heart. Therefore I will find favor, good understanding and high esteem in the sight of God and man. Even as You made Daniel to find favor, compassion and lovingkindness with man because he would not defile himself, I believe You also cause me to find favor with God and man. Because I diligently seek good, I know I am seeking God's favor. Thank You Father, that You bless me and watch over me, guarding and keeping me; You make Your face to shine upon and enlighten me. You are gracious, kind, and merciful, giving me peace and tranquility of heart and life continually. You have put Your Name upon me and You have blessed me. As Esther obtained favor in the sight of all who looked upon her, so do I in the Name of Jesus, for Lord, You are no respecter of persons.

Study: Prov 3:3-4; Dan 1:8,9; Prov 11:27; Num 6:24-25; Esth 2:15

Godly Counsel

Listen to counsel and receive instruction, That you may be wise in your latter days. There are many plans in a man's heart, Nevertheless the LORD*'s counsel — that will stand.* Prov 19:20-21

We are blessed because we do not walk and live in the counsel of the ungodly, following their advice, plans   and purposes. Nor do we stand submissive and inactive in the path where sinners walk, nor do we sit down to relax and rest where the scornful and mockers gather. But our delight and desire are in the law of the Lord, and in Your Word we meditate day and night. Therefore we are like trees, planted by the rivers of water, bringing forth our fruit in its season. Our leaf also does not wither, and whatever we do prospers.

Lord, You give us skillful and godly wisdom; from Your mouth we receive knowledge and understanding. Thank You that You hide away sound and godly wisdom and store it for the righteous. You are a shield for those who walk uprightly and in integrity, that You may guard the paths of justice. You preserve our way.

I believe that we heed instruction and correction and therefore we are not only ourselves in the way of life, but a way of life for others. We do not neglect or refuse reproof, so we will not go astray or cause others to err toward a path of ruin.

Study: Ps 1:1-3; Prov 2:6-8; Prov 10:17

Power of Indwelling Spirit

"Strengthened with might through His Spirit in the inner man" Eph 3:16

I am a child of God, I belong to Jesus. I have overcome and defeated the agents of the antichrist, because He that lives in me is greater than he that is in the world. My body is the temple of the Holy Spirit; it is His sanctuary and He has permanent dwelling in me. He will never leave me nor forsake me.

Jesus has given me all power and authority to trample upon serpents and scorpions, and physical and mental strength and ability to overcome all the powers that the enemy possesses and nothing shall in any way harm me. These attesting signs shall accompany me. In Jesus' Name I drive out demons and speak with new tongues. If I pick up serpents or drink anything deadly, it shall not harm me. I will lay my hands on the sick, and they shall recover. You will work with me Lord, confirming the Word preached with signs and wonders following.

I am assured that because I steadfastly believe in You, Jesus, I will be able to do the things that You did and even greater works because You are with the Father. You will grant whatever I may ask in Your Name in acccordance with Your will so that the Father may be glorified in and through the Son.

Study: 1 John 4:4; 1 Cor 6:19; Heb 13:5; Luke 10:19; Mark 16:17-20; John 14:12-13

Holiness

Create in me a clean heart, O God, And renew a steadfast spirit within me.
Ps 51:10

Thank You Father, in Jesus' Name, for the abundance of Your grace that has come and delivered me from all sin. Your grace trains me to reject and renounce all ungodliness, and worldly passionate desires, so that I may live a discreet, temperate, self-controlled and upright life in this present world.

The God of Peace Himself sanctifies me through and through by separating me from profane things to make me pure and wholly consecrated to You. I will behave myself wisely in a mature way. I will walk within my house with a perfect heart, and will set nothing wicked before my eyes.

I present my body a living sacrifice, holy and acceptable to You Lord, which is my reasonable service. I will not be conformed to this world but be transformed by the renewing of my mind, proving what is that good and acceptable and perfect will of God. Not my will, but Yours be done, O Lord.

I will not touch the unclean thing, but cleanse myself of all the filthiness of the flesh and spirit, perfecting holiness in the fear of God. I do not walk after the counsel of the ungodly, nor stand in the way of sinners, nor sit in the seat of the scornful, but my delight is in Your law, O Lord, and in Your Word do I meditate day and night.

Unto me are all things pure, for in You I am pure. As I behold the Word of God, I am being transformed into Your image, from glory to glory.

Study: Titus 2:11-12; 1 Thes 5:23; Ps 101:2; Rom 12:1-2; Luke 22:42; 2 Cor 6:17; 2 Cor 7:1; Ps 1:1-2; Titus 1:5; 2 Cor 3:18

Obedience

Has the Lord as great delight in burnt offerings and sacrifices, As in obeying the voice of the Lord? Behold, to obey is better than sacrifice.
1 Sam 15:22

Father, You have set before me this day life and death, blessing and cursing. I choose life that I may live. I will walk in obedience to Your Word all the days of my life. No curse is able to overtake me. It is better to obey than to sacrifice, for rebellion is as the sin of witchcraft and stubbornness is as iniquity and idolatry.

Because I am obedient and willing before You, I thank You that I shall eat of the good of the land. I do love You Lord, therefore I keep Your commands. I thank You that because I obey Your commands (Your laws, testimonies and statutes), You will manifest Yourself to me.

I am a doer of Your Word and not just a hearer. I will not deceive my own self. I study Your Word and am eager to present myself to God, approved (tested by trial), a workman who has no cause to be ashamed, correctly analyzing and accurately dividing (rightly handling and skillfully teaching) the Word of Truth.

I delight to do Your will, O Lord.

Study: Deut 30:19; Is 1:19; James 1:22; 2 Tim 2:15; Ps 40:8

Entering The Secret Place of God

He who dwells in the secret place of the Most High Shall abide under the shadow of the Almighty. Ps 91:1

Lord, I come to You because I want to know You. I want to have a deep and personal relationship with You. I want to know the mysteries that pertain to Your Kingdom, O Lord. Your word says that You will instruct and teach me in the way I should go; You will counsel me and give me understanding.

I desire to walk closer to You every day; to hear Your voice and to know Your desires, Your plans and Your will for me. Draw me into that inner place; that inner chamber within me, that You call the Secret Place, where You will meet with me and where I can meet with You.

Lord, like King David, who entered into Your presence with worship and singing, I calm my soul (my mind, will and emotions), drawing away from the cares of this world to meet with You. I know that You have great wisdom and revelation and in that secret place within me I will find perfect peace and joy.

God, You created a secret place for Moses in the mountain so he could get a glimpse of Your Glory. He received understanding, instruction, direction, comfort, and revelation in that place. I desire to enter into that inner place today and always. I ask for Your healing touch in my life as I sit quietly before You. Show me the things that are blocking me from walking closer to You Lord. Open my ears to hear Your voice and my eyes to see as You see.

You say that I am to come to You and lay all my burdens at Your feet and You will give me rest. I come to You and lay all my worries, sorrows, fears, doubts, and unbelief before You. Forgive me for not trusting You. It is the upright, the honest, the fair, the wise, and those with integrity who can enter into Your confidence. Cleanse me today so I can walk closer to You. Give me the wisdom to walk in a way that is pleasing to You.

Today I purpose to spend more quiet time with You so I can dwell in that place of safety and closeness. It is in that place that You will be "More than enough" and prove Yourself to be a God of super abundant provision.

I trust You Lord and honour You in all Your ways. Speak to me Lord, I am listening! Instruct me, guide me, heal me, encourage me and like Habakkuk I will write down all You say to me so that I can look back and read and remember "How great is my God". Thank You Lord for all You are doing in my life. Thank You for being my Lord and Saviour.

Study: Ps 32:8; Matt 6:6; Ex 33:18-23; Matt 11:28-29; Prov 3:32; Ps 24:4; Ps 84:11; Ps 25:14; Hab 2:2

Chapter Six

FRUIT OF THE SPIRIT

Love

Beloved, let us love one another, for love is of God; and everyone who loves is born of God and knows God. 1 John 4:7

Father, because Your love is shed abroad in my heart by the Holy Spirit, I endure long and am patient and kind. I never boil over with jealousy, nor am I envious. I am not boastful or vainglorious, nor do I display myself haughtily. Because of Your love in me, I am not conceited, arrogant or inflated with pride. I am not rude or unmannerly and I do not act unbecomingly.

Your agape love in me does not insist on its own rights or its own way, for it is not self-seeking. I am not touchy, fretful or resentful. I take no acount of the evil done to me and pay no attention to a suffered wrong. I do not rejoice at injustice and unrighteousness, but rejoice when right and truth prevail.

I bear up under anything and everything that comes. I am ever ready to believe the best of every person. My hopes are fadeless under all circumstances and I endure everything without weakening. You have said that love never fails, so I thank You because the fruit of love is operating freely in my life, I never fail. Thank You for Your love in my life, in Jesus' Name.

Study: Rom 5:5; 1 Cor 13:4-8

Joy

These things I have spoken to you, that My joy may remain in you, and that your joy may be full. John 15:11

Father, Your kingdom is not meat and drink, but righteousness, peace and joy in the Holy Ghost. He that serves God in this manner is approved of God and acceptable to man. I thank You that the joy of the Lord is my strength. I have a heart that is happy, which is good medicine, and I possess a cheerful mind which works healing in my life.

I will rejoice, delight and gladden myself always in You Lord. I delight to do Your will, O God! I have found Your Words and I do eat them daily. Your Word is to me the joy and rejoicing of my heart.

I will continue in Your Word. I will put on Your beautiful garments of praise, shaking off the bonds of fear, defeat, inferiority or weakness.

As I walk in joy and rejoice daily in You, I thank You that there is a supernatural hedge of protection round about me. I am delivered from the hands of my enemies. As Jehoshaphat and his people sang their way to deliverance and were joyful and jubilant, so I will rejoice in You. I release Your joy in my life and thank You for delivering me from the hand of my enemies, in Jesus' Name.

Study: Rom 14: 17-18; Neh. 8:10; Prov 17:22; Phil 4:4; Jer 15:16; Is 61:3; 2 Chr. 20:22-30

Peace

*Peace I leave with you, My peace I give to you; not as the world gives
do I give to you. Let not your heart be troubled, neither let it be afraid.*
John 14:27

Father, in Jesus' Name I thank You for Your covenant of peace
and mercy today. I do not fret or have worry or anxiety about
anything, but in every circumstance by prayer and supplication,
with thanksgiving, I let my requests be made known unto You.
Your peace (that tranquil state of a soul assured of its salvation) is
mine. So, fearing nothing from God and content with my earthly
lot of whatever sort that is, that peace that transcends all
understanding will garrison and guard over my heart and mind
through Christ Jesus. I will speak and think only upon
whatsoever is worthy, and honorable, whatever is just, whatever
is pure, lovely and lovable, whatever is kind and winsome and
gracious. If there is any virtue and excellence, if there is anything
worthy of praise, I will think upon and take account of these
things. Thank You Father, that the effect of righteousness shall be
peace, internal and external and the result of righteousness,
quietness and confident trust forever. I believe I shall dwell in a
peaceable habitation, in safe dwellings and in quiet resting
places.

For though the mountains should depart and the hills be
removed, yet Your love and kindness, O Lord, shall not depart
from me, nor shall Your covenant of peace and completeness be
removed. Because I establish myself in righteousness (right in
conformity with God's will and order) I shall be far from
thoughts of oppression or destruction, for I shall not fear. I shall
be far from terror for it shall not come near me. Because I hearken
to wisdom I shall dwell securely and in confident trust. Because I
love Your law, great peace is mine and nothing shall offend me
or make me stumble.

You, my God, have not given me a spirit of fear, but of power, love and a sound mind. You are my Shepherd. I fear no evil, for You are with me. The chastisement of my peace was upon Jesus and You have given me His peace. In the world I will have tribulation, but I am of good cheer, for Jesus has overcome the world!

Study: Is 54:10; Phil 4:6-8; Is 32: 17,18; Is 54: 10-14; Prov 1:33; Ps 119:165; 2 Tim 1:7; Ps 23:1-4; John 16:33

Longsuffering

For you have need of endurance, so that after you have done the will of God, you may receive the promise. Heb 10:35

Heavenly Father, I thank You that You are merciful and gracious, longsuffering and abundant in goodness and truth. Your nature now abides in me and I acknowledge that I am longsuffering, being of good temperament and patient. Because love lives in me, I suffer long. I count it all joy when I fall into, or encounter trials or various temptations, knowing that the trial of my faith brings out endurance, steadfastness and patience. I let patience do a thorough work in me so that I may be perfectly and fully developed, with no defects, lacking in nothing.

Seeing that I am surrounded with so great a cloud of witnesses, I run with patient endurance and steady active persistence, the appointed course that is set before me, laying aside every unnecessary weight, and that sin which so readily entangles me.

With Your help Lord, I will walk worthy of the calling with which I am called, with all lowliness and gentleness, with longsuffering, bearing with others in love, endeavoring to keep the unity of the Spirit in the bond of peace. As the elect of God, I put on tender mercies, kindness, humbleness of mind, meekness and longsuffering, bearing with and forgiving others even as Christ also forgives me.

Study: Ex 34:6; 1 Cor 13:4; James 1:2-4; Heb 12:1; Eph 4:1-3; Col 3:12,13

Gentleness

*Therefore, as the elect of God, holy and beloved, put on tender mercies,
kindness, humility, meekness, longsuffering; bearing with one another, and
forgiving one another.* Col 3:12

I thank You heavenly Father, that the fruit of the Spirit You have placed in me is gentleness. As the servant of the Lord, I must not be in strife, but will be gentle unto all men, apt to teach and patient. I will correct my opponents with courtesy and gentleness, in the hope that God may grant that they will repent and come to know the Truth. I put on a heart of compassion, kindness, humility, gentleness and patience. Your gentleness, O Lord, makes me great. I walk with the wisdom that is from above, which is first pure, then peaceable, gentle, willing to yield, full of mercy and good fruits, without partiality and without hypocrisy. I will be wise as a serpent and gentle as a dove and lowly of heart, and I find rest unto my soul.

Study: Gal 5:22; 2 Tim. 2:24-25; Col 3:12; Ps 18:35; James 3:17; Matt 10:16

Goodness

A good man out of the good treasure of his heart brings forth good things.
Matt 12:35

Father, I rejoice in You and in the knowledge that the earth is full of Your goodness and lovingkindness. I consider and give attentive, continuous care to watching over others, studying how I may stir them up to love, helpful deeds and noble activities. Thank You Father, that Your goodness flows through me, for the fruit of the Spirit is in all goodness, righteousness and truth. You have created me in Christ Jesus unto good works which You have predestined for me to walk in them.

Thank You that I walk worthy of You unto all pleasing, being fruitful in every good work and increasing in the knowledge of God. I will let my light freely shine before all men that they may see my good works and glorify You. I will not render evil for evil unto any man, but will ever follow that which is good. I will walk humbly before You, allowing Your goodness to flow freely through me. Your goodness and mercy will follow me all the days of my life, in Jesus' Name.

Study: Ps 33:5; Heb 10:24; Eph5:9; Eph 2:10; Col 1:10; Matt 5:16; 1 Thes 5:15; Mic 6:8; Ps 23:6

Faithfulness

Well done, good and faithful servant; you were faithful over a few things, I will make you ruler over many things. Matt 25:21

Father, I thank You that I am saved by grace, through faith, and that faithfulness (loyalty, constancy, reliability and steadfastness) are evident in my life. Your tender mercies and lovingkindness keep me from being consumed. They are new every morning. Great is Your faithfulness. I thank You that I am a faithful servant, and pray You will find me faithful at Your return.

I will not forsake or neglect to assemble together with other believers, but will admonish (warning, urging and encouraging) others, and all the more faithfully as I see the day approaching. I confess faithfulness, for You have promised that one who is faithful shall abound with blessings.

Study: Eph 2:8; Lam. 3:22-23; Matt 24:45-46; Heb 10:25; Prov 28:20

Meekness

Now the man Moses was very humble, more than all men who were on the face of the earth. Num 12:3

Father, thank You for helping me to walk in meekness (mildness, forbearance, the state of being submissive and humble), possessing a total dependence on You. I come to You with all my labors and receive Your rest, allowing Your ease to relieve and refresh my soul. I take Your yoke (which is easy) upon me and Your burden (which is light) also, in order that I may learn of You and become like You.

I pray that You would increase in me and I would decrease. I follow after Your example by serving others and giving my life for them, instead of seeking to be served. I let the mind of Christ be in me, doing nothing out of selfish ambition or conceit, but in lowliness of mind esteeming others better than myself. I do not look to my own interests, but also for the interests of others. I do not set my mind on high things, but associate with the humble, not being wise in my own opinion. I confess that I am submissive to others and clothed with humility. God resists the proud but gives grace to the humble. Therefore, I humble myself under the mighty hand of God that You may exalt me in due time. I receive the engrafted Word of God with a teachable spirit, for it is able to save my soul. I pray that I may always be ready to give an answer to everyone who asks me a reason of the hope that is within me with meekness and fear.

Study: Matt 11:28-30; John 3:30; Phil 2:3-5; Rom 12:16; 1 Pet. 5:5-6; Jam 1:21; 1 Pet. 3:15

Self-Control

*Whoever has no rule over his own spirit Is like a city broken down,
without walls.* Prov 25:28

Father God, I press toward the mark for the prize of the high calling
of God in Christ Jesus. As I strive for mastery in all things, I pray that
the fruit of self-control would be exercised in my life. I pray that I
may always be quick to hear, slow to speak, for man's anger does not
promote the righteousness of God. I give all diligence to add to my
faith, virtue, to virtue knowledge, to knowledge self-control, to self-
control perseverance, to perseverance godliness, to godliness
brotherly kindness and to brotherly kindness love. For since these
are mine and abound, I will be neither barren nor unfruitful in the
knowledge of my Lord Jesus Christ.

I pray for strength so that I would abstain from the sensual urges
and passions of my flesh that wage war against my soul. I am slow
to anger, knowing that it is better than being mighty, and I rule my
own spirit, which is superior to taking a city. I realize that the
discretion of a man makes him slow to anger and it is my glory to
overlook a transgression.

Study: Phil 3:14; 1 Cor 9:25; James 1:19-20; 1 Pet. 1:5-8; 1 Pet 2:11; Prov 16:32;
Prov 19:11

Chapter Seven

PRAYERS FOR FREEDOM

Redemption

Let the redeemed of the Lord say so, whom He has redeemed from the hand of the enemy. Ps 107:2

Thank You Father that I am redeemed. You have delivered and drawn me to Yourself out of the control of the dominion of Satan. I thank You Lord, that I have a new King and I belong to a new Kingdom. Thank You Jesus, for purchasing my freedom from the curse of the law's condemnation by becoming a curse for me. As it is written: "Cursed is everyone who hangs on a tree." Now, because I am in Christ, I am a new creature altogether. I am a new species, the kind that never existed before. The old moral and spiritual condition has passed away. Behold, the new has come.

Study: Col 1:13; Gal 3:13; 2 Cor 5:17

Cleansing for Sensitive Conscience

The purpose of the commandment is love from a pure heart, from a good conscience, and from sincere faith. 1 Tim 1:5

Thank You Father, that in You I have redemption, deliverance and salvation through the blood of Jesus. I have the remission of my offenses in accordance with the riches and the generosity of Your grace and favor. As I walk in the light as You are in the light I have true unbroken fellowship with my brothers and sisters.

The blood of Jesus continually removes all guile and cleanses me from all sin.

I am reconciled in peace unto You through the blood. I thank You Father, that You have chosen, con-secrated, sanctified me and made me holy through the blood of Jesus. May peace and grace be given me in increasing abundance, freedom from fears, and freedom from agitating passions and moral conflicts. I know I am sealed and the covenant ratified through the blood of Jesus. Let the blood now purify my conscience from dead works and lifeless observances to serve and worship the living God. In Jesus' Name.

Study: Eph 1:7; 1John 1:7; Col 1:20; Heb 9:14

Repentance

For godly sorrow produces repentance leading to salvation, not to be regretted. 2 Cor 7:10

Heavenly Father, I come before You in the Name of Jesus, in obedience to Your Word to repent of sin. Your Word says that no one can serve two masters. I turn from my sin and acknowledge it before You. (Name it) I confess it and thank You that You are faithful and just to forgive me and cleanse me from all unrighteousness.

Sin shall not have dominion over me. There is therefore now no condemantion to me, for I am in Christ Jesus and walk not after the flesh but after the Spirit. The law of the Spirit of life in Christ Jesus has made me free from the law of sin and death.

Thank You for helping me to remain sensitive to the leading of the Holy Spirit and His correction. Thank You Lord, that my life brings forth fruit that is consistent with repentance and proves my change of heart. Thank You Father for the wealth of Your goodness, kindness, forbearance and longsuffering in my life that has led me to repentance. I change my mind and inner man to accept Your will.

My heart will remain tender and pliable in Your sight. I pray I will never be hardened by the effects of sin. I will walk closely with You. I receive Your forgiveness by faith, according to Your Word.

Study: Matt 6:24; 1 John 1:9; Rom 6:14; Rom 8:1-2; Matt 3:8; Rom 2:4; Heb 3:13

Righteousness

For with the heart one believes unto righteousness, and with the mouth confession is made unto salvation. Rom 10:10

Father, thank You for the gift of righteousness (my right standing with God in Christ Jesus). I have received Your overflowing grace (unmerited favor) and righteousness and reign as a king through Jesus Christ in this life.

Thank You for Jesus, who personally took my sins in His own body on the cross that I might die to sin and live unto righteousness. Thank You that Jesus was not sent into the world to condemn it but that through Him we might find salvation. For my sake, He was made to be sin (who knew no sin) that I might be made the righteousness of God in Him.

Thank You that I am justified by the blood of Christ and have been brought into a right relationship with You. Thank You for this wonderful gift, in Jesus' Name.

Study: Rom 5:17; 1 Pet 2:24; John 3:16-17; 2 Cor 5:21; Rom 3:21-24; 2 Cor 9:15

Freedom from Condemnation and Fear

There is therefore now no condemnation to those who are in Christ Jesus,
who do not walk according to the flesh, but according to the Spirit.
Rom 8:1

Heavenly Father, I rejoice knowing that You have delivered me from the power of darkness and translated me into the kingdom of Your dear Son. Your perfect, full-grown and complete love casts out all fear from my heart and life. Your perfect love grows in me, maturing in my life so that fear can no longer torment me.

You have established me in righteousness. I am far from oppression, for I shall not fear; and from terror, for it shall not come near me. I sought You, Lord, and You heard me and delivered me from all my fears.

Thank You that even though I walk through the valley of the shadow of death I fear no evil, for You are always with me. I will not fear, I will not be dismayed, for You are my God, You strengthen me, You help me. You uphold me with Your righteous right hand. Fear and dread, in Jesus' Name, I resist you! I have not been given a spirit of fear, but a spirit of power, of love and a sound mind. The Lord is my Light and my salvation, whom shall I fear? He is the strength of my life, of whom shall I be afraid? Because I listen to the Lord, I dwell safely, and am secure, without fear of evil, in Jesus' Name.

Study: Col 1:13; 1 John 4:18; Is 54:14; Ps 34:4; Ps 23:4; Is 41:10; 2 Tim. 1:7; Ps 27:1; Prov 1:33

Freedom From the Past, Bad Memories, and Condemnation

Forgetting those things which are behind and reaching forward to those things which are ahead, I press toward the goal for the prize of the upward call of God in Christ Jesus. Phil 3:13-14

Dear Father, You have ordained peace, favor and blessing (temporal and spiritual) for us, for You have wrought in us and for us all our works. O Lord our God, other masters beside You have ruled over us but we will acknowledge and mention Your Name only. The former tyrant masters are dead. They shall not live and reappear. They are powerless ghosts. They shall not rise and come back. Therefore, You have made an end of them and caused every memory of them, every trace of their supremacy to perish. One thing I do, forgetting what lies behind and straining forward to what lies ahead, I press on toward the goal to win the supreme and heavenly prize of God in Christ Jesus.

Thank You Father, that I have redemption through the blood of Christ. I am redeemed from the curse of the law's condemnation by Christ, who became a curse for me, and have found and secured a complete redemption. I freely admit that I have sinned and confess my sin. You are faithful and just, true to Your own nature and promises, and forgive my sins, continually cleansing me from all unrighteousness.

Study: Is 26: 12-14; Phil 3:13-14; Col 1:14; Gal 3:13; 1 John 1:9

Breaking Generational Curses

Lord, even the demons are subject to us in Your Name. Luke 10:17

Father, I thank You that You have given me the keys of the kingdom of Heaven, and whatever I bind on earth will be bound in heaven, and whatever I loose on earth will be loosed in heaven.

Therefore, in the Name of Jesus, the Name that is above every name and ALL things, I bind up every unclean spirit and assignment coming against me, (my children, family) from, or by, or through anyone or anything, named or unnamed, known or unknown, and from generations back. In the Name of Jesus I bind up the principalities, powers, rulers of the darkness of this world, spiritual wickedness and hosts in high places, and the prince of the power of the air. I bind up the strongman and stronghold, the spirit of antichrist, every evil spirit and plague, the spirit of confusion, illusion and delusion in the Name of Jesus. I renounce anything to do with witchcraft, horoscopes or anything to do with the powers of darkness.

In Jesus' Name, I bind up the spirit of infirmity, sickness, disease, pain, addiction, affliction, calamity, the devourer, the destroyer, the accuser, the deceiver, the corrupter, and every spirit of poverty that has been passes down to me by generational curses. I break off the curse of addiction from my life - addiction to food, alcohol, drugs and any other deadly thing in Jesus' Name! I say I am free from the generational curses upon my family. I am a new person in Christ Jesus, and none of these belong to me or my family. I break their power now in Jesus' Name!!!!

In the Name of Jesus, I bind up the spirit of strife and division, back biting and gossip, critical and judgmental spirits, spirits of resistance and hindrance, every spirit of retribution, revenge and retaliation, and the lying, seducing, deceiving spirits of deception. In the Name of Jesus I bind up every root of fear, doubt, unbelief, discouragement and every deadly thing from despair to depression; the spirit of pride, rebellion, disobedience, self, ego, independence, bitterness, and the lust of the flesh.

I rebuke you UNCLEAN SPIRITS. I loose, in the Name of Jesus Christ, deliverance, freedom and liberation, peace, joy, hope, gladness of heart, love, healing and wholeness, mercy and grace, blessings and favor, restoration of the years that the locusts have eaten, the resurrection power of Jesus Christ, a mighty harvest, and a boldness to witness for Christ in Jesus' Name. Every family curse is broken and I am FREE! Amen and Amen!!

Study: Matt 16:19; Matt 18:18; Phil 2:9-10; Eph 1:20-23; 2 Cor 5:17; 1 Tim 4:1-2; Jude 9; Zec 3:2; Joel 2:25

Healing

I believe in the healing power of God. Cancer (or any other sickness or disease) can be beaten! You can beat it to death with the all-powerful Word of the Living God!

God's words contain inherent within them the capacity, the energy, the life to produce healing in your body. The Word must penetrate your spirit where life is deposited and healing is appropriated. Psalm 103:2,3 says, "Bless the Lord, O my soul, and forget not all His benefits: Who forgives all your iniquities, who heals all your diseases." In the Basic English Bible it quotes that verse, "He takes away all your diseases."

Psalm 107:20 says, "He sent His Word and healed them, and delivered them from their destructions." The Moffat translation says, "He sent His Word to heal them and preserve their life." Proverbs 4:20-22 says, "My son, attend to my words; incline your ear to my sayings; do not let them depart from your eyes; keep them in the midst of your heart. For they are life unto those that find them, and health to all their flesh." The

Living Bible says, "Let them penetrate deep within your heart." Knox translation says, "Let a man master them; they will bring life and healing to his whole being." Rotherham says, ". . . to every part of one's flesh they bring healing."

Exodus 15:25 says, "I, the Lord, am your physician." Jesus is our great physician and He gives a prescription for healing. A regular medical doctor also hands out prescriptions and we diligently have them filled, pay lots of money and faithfully take them as directed on the label and give them weeks to work. Let's do the same with God's medicine. Let's take as the Word directs us in Proverbs 4:20-22 and consistently, faithfully apply the Word to our hearts: meditating on it, pondering it, reading it out loud, memorizing it and giving it time to penetrate our spirits. Head knowledge will not work.

Here are some healing confessions based on God's Word. Say them out loud, over and over until healing is appropriated. Don't take health for granted but quote from these confessions every day. Keep your body healed, in Jesus' Name.

Healing Confessions

From Exodus 23:25; Jeremiah 1:11; Matthew 8:17 and I Peter 2:24. I worship You Lord, and thank You for blessing my food and water and taking sickness and disease away from the midst of me. Thank You Lord, for watching over Your Word to perform it. Sickness and disease, Jesus took my infirmities and bore my sicknesses and by His stripes I was healed. Go sickness, go disease, in Jesus' Name. You have no place here.

From Exodus 15:25-26, I John 1:9, Jeremiah 1:11, Matthew 8:17. Lord Jesus, I dedicate myself to hearken to Your voice and to keep Your Word. I thank You I am cleansed from all sin by the blood of Jesus. You are Jehovah Raphe, the Lord that healeth me. You are healing me now. Thank You Father, in Jesus' Name. You watch over Your Word to perform it. You are my healer. Thank

You that Jesus took my infirmities and bore my sicknesses, and I am forever delivered from them.

From Psalm 91:1-6, 10, 16; Isaiah 55:11, Malachi 4:1. I am sitting under the secret protection of the Most High and I am resting under the shadow of the Almighty. I say of the Lord, "You are my refuge and my fortress, in You will I put my trust." You will surely deliver me from all the enemy's snares. You are Jehovah Raphe, the God that heals me and Jesus has taken sickness and disease away from me. Your Word never returns void; You watch over it to fulfill it. I am not afraid of sickness and disease, which are snares of the enemy, because You are right now delivering me. Your Word is my shield and buckler against any and every sickness and disease and they are forbidden to come near me in Jesus' Name.

Confession: You forgive all of my iniquities and You heal all my diseases. You are healing me now. Healing is a benefit of being one of Your children. I am a child of Abraham and the promises of Abraham are mine. Healing is your children's bread. Healing is my bread and I receive it now. Sickness and disease, I command you to leave my body now. My body is the temple of the Holy Ghost and I command all viruses, all infirmities, all diseases (name it) to leave this temple now, in Jesus' Name.

Confession: The power of death and life are in my tongue (Prov 19:21). I speak wise words that heal me now. God's promises are wise words and I confess them, in Jesus' Name. Jesus is the Lord that heals me now. Life is in me because greater is He that is in me than he that is in the world (I John 4:4). I say, "I am healed, in Jesus' name." I say, "I will not die, but live and declare the works of the Lord." (Psalm 118:17). My tongue makes me well. I command every cell, tissue, organ and muscle in my body to obey the Word of the Lord and be healed, in Jesus' name. I say, "Jesus is purifying my blood now, every drop of it. Jesus is my healer and I receive my healing now, in Jesus' Name."

Confession: I thank You Lord that You loved me so much that you gave yourself for me; that You were wounded for my transgressions and bruised for my iniquities. I rejoice in knowing that You Yourself took my infirmities and carried my diseases and that by Your stripes I was healed! I thank You Lord that because of what You did for me on the Cross of Calvary, the sanctuary of my body has become a hostile environment to germs, sicknesses, diseases, cancers, and demons. I give no place to sickness in my life, but I resist it and in Jesus' Name I command it to flee far from me. Thank You Lord, that by Your grace I walk in divine health today.

Study: Isa 53:5; Matt 8:17; 1 Cor 6:19; Ps 103:3; Matt 4:24; Jam 4:7; 3 John 2

Prosperity

Let the LORD be magnified, Who has pleasure in the prosperity of His servant. Ps 35:27

Father, I rejoice in Your will for me to prosper, even as my soul (my mind, will and emotions) prosper in Your Word. I will say continually, "Let the Lord be magnified, who has pleasure in the prosperity of His servant." You have given me the power to get wealth that You may establish Your covenant with me in the earth. I thank You that as I meditate in Your Word day and night and learn how to be a doer of it, I will make my way prosperous and have good success. For You are the Lord who teaches me to profit and leads me in the way I should go.

1I seek You and Your kingdom first. I thank You that all the things I need will be added unto me. You have already given me the gift of Your own Son to accomplish my salvation and will continue to freely and richly give me all things that pertain to life and godliness, that I may prosper in my physical and spiritual life.

You are my shepherd and I shall not want, for they that seek You shall not want or lack any good thing. You supply all my needs according to Your riches in glory through Christ Jesus. Even now, as I hear and do Your Word, You have commanded blessings to overtake me and come upon my storehouse (bank account) and upon all that I set my hand to do. I shall lend to many and not borrow, for You have made me the head and not the tail; I am above only and not beneath and I thank You for it. Your right hand has held me up and Your gentleness has made me great.

I honor You Lord, with my substance and the first of all my increase. I cheerfully bring all the tithes into Your storehouse and thank You for opening the windows of heaven and pouring out so great a blessing that I have no place to keep it but have over and above what I asked or thought, to give again into Your kingdom. With the same generosity that I have given, others will give to me in good measure, pressed down, shaken together and running over.

You have already rebuked the devourer for my sake and now I take the authority You have given me in Jesus' Name and bind every device and plan of the devil sent against prosperity in any area of my life, physically, spiritually, emotionally and materially.

I praise You Father, that Your covenant with me will never be broken and that You do not alter any of the words You have spoken. Your Word will not return void but is prospering on my behalf in all that You sent it to do. Thank You for Your angels who excel in strength. They hearken unto the voice of Your Word as I have spoken it, and are even now going forth to minister for me. Because I am an heir of salvation, You are causing blessings to come upon me as You have commanded.

Study: 3 John 1:2; Ps 35:27; Deut 8:18; Josh. 1:8; Is 48:17; Matt 6:33; Rom 8:32; 2 Pet 1:3; Ps 23:1; Ps 34:10; Phil 4:19; Deut 28:1-14; Prov 3:9; Mal. 3:9-10; Eph 3:20; Luke 6:38; Mal. 3:11; Ps 89:34; Is 55:11; Ps 103:20; Heb 1:14

Prayer for Giving

Let each one give as he purposes in his heart, not grudgingly or of necessity;
for God loves a cheerful giver. 2 Cor 9:7

Father God, I so desire to be set free to give and be a channel through which Your blessings may flow. In the Name of Jesus, loose me from a covetous spirit and the spirit of greed or selfishness, and grant unto me the gift of giving, that my giving may increase to further Your kingdom and win precious souls.

Father God, I do not want to rob or defraud You. Therefore, I will continue to bring all the tithes (the whole tenth of my income) into the storehouse, which is my local church, that there may be food in Your house, and that I may be blessed with a blessing. You said, "Prove Me in this" so I prove You now by it. Open the window of heaven for me and pour out a blessing that there be not room enough to receive it. I will not consume it upon my own lusts but I will continue to be a blessing to others.

Father, I thank You that You will rebuke the devourer for my sake, that he will not destroy the fruit of my ground, neither diminish the means of my income. People shall call me happy and blessed; for I shall be as a delightful land, bringing You glory, my precious Father.

Father, You have also taught me to give over and above the tithe (to missionaries, building funds, to the education of Your little ones, to television outreaches and other ministry). As I do this, Your Word says that gifts will be given unto me, good measure, pressed down into my wallet. According to Your promise, Lord, with the measure I have dealt out it will be measured back to me so I may continue to give, and be a blessing for Your honor and glory, O Lord, my God.

All that I have is Yours, O Lord. Continue to pour through me prosperity (spiritually and materially) that others may be blessed and saved. In Jesus' Name.

Study: Mal. 3:8-12; James 4:3; Luke 6:38

Tithing

Of all that You give me I will surely give a tenth to You. Gen 28:22

Father, I thank and praise You for delivering me and drawing me unto Yourself, out of the control and dominion of darkness, and transferring me into the kingdom of the Son of Your love. Thank You for bringing me out of the land of bondage with a mighty hand and an outstretched arm to a land flowing with milk and honey.

I now bring before You the firstfruits of the increase which You have given me. I bring it before Your presence, and set it down and worship You, Lord. I bring the tithe before You according to Your commandment. I have not eaten it in my mourning (making it unclean) nor have I handled any of it in an unclean way or given it to the dead (ungodly). I have listened and understood Your Word and have done according to all that You have spoken.

Thank You now for Your blessings upon me. You have brought me into a land that flows with milk and honey. I bring my tithe to the ministers of Your Word that You have appointed here in the earth to receive them. Father, I do not want to rob or defraud You. Therefore, I will continue to bring all the tithes (the whole tenth of my income) into the storehouse, which is my local church, that there may be food in Your house, and that I may receive Your great blessing.

You said, "Prove Me in this," so I prove You now. Open the windows of heaven for me and pour out a blessing that there may not be room enough to receive it. I will not consume it upon my own lusts, but continue to be a blessing to others. Thank You for rebuking the devourer for my sake, that he will not destroy the fruit of my ground, neither diminish the source of my income. People shall call me happy and blessed, for I shall be like a delightful land. I honor You Lord, with my capital and sufficiency and the firstfruits of all my increase, from my righteous labors, and I receive Your blessing upon my storage places, my bank accounts and my house, that they may be filled with plenty and overflowing. Thank You Father, for blessing my faithful and consistent obedience to bring the tithe to You, in Jesus' Name.

Study: Col 1:13; Deut 26:8-15; Mal. 3:8-12; Prov 3:9-10; Deut 28:8

Success

The man began to prosper, and continued prospering until he became very prosperous. Gen 26:13

Heavenly Father, I thank You that Your desire and plan for my life is to be successful. I will not allow Your Word to depart from my mouth, but will meditate on it day and night, that I may observe and pay attention to do according to all that is written in it. As I do this, I will make my way prosperous and I shall deal wisely and have good success.

I hide Your Word in my heart so that I will not sin against You. I study and am eager to do my utmost to present myself approved (tested by trial) unto You as a workman that has no cause to be ashamed, correctly analyzing and accurately dividing [rightly handling and skillfully teaching] the Word of Truth.

Father, I hear Your Word and do it. I labor diligently to build my house upon the rock and not the sand, so that when the storms and floods come and beat on my house, it shall not fall but continue to reside in its place. I am a doer of Your Word and not just a hearer only. I will abide (dwell and reside) in You and allow Your Words to abide in me. Thus, I know that whatever I ask shall be done, in Jesus' Name.

Study: Josh. 1:8; Ps 119:11; 2 Tim 2:15; Matt 7:24-25; James 1:22; John 15:7

Employment

He shall be like a tree planted by the rivers of water, that brings forth its fruit in its season, whose leaf also shall not wither; and whatever he does shall prosper. Ps 1:3

Father, in Jesus' Name, I believe and confess Your Word today, knowing that You watch over it to perform it. Your Word prospers in me. You are my source for every need, comfort and encouragement. My desire is to owe no man anything but to love him. Therefore, I am strong. Let not my hands be weak or slack, for my work shall be rewarded. My wages are not counted as a favor or a gift, but as something owed to me.

I make it my ambition to live quietly and peacefully, minding my own affairs and working with my hands. I am correct and honorable and command the respect of the outside world; being self-supporting, independent and having need of nothing. You, supply all my needs according to Your riches in glory by Christ Jesus.

I learn to apply myself to good deeds, to honest labor and honorable employment, so that I am able to meet necessary demands whenever the occasion may require. You have set before me a wide open door which no one can shut. I do not fear and am not dismayed, for You, Father, strengthen me. You help me and in Jesus I have perfect peace and confidence.

Because I delight in Your Word, meditating in it day and night, everything I do prospers.

Study: Jer 1:12; Rom 13:8; Rom 4:4; 1 Thess. 4:11,12; Phil 4:19; 2 Thess. 3:8;
Rev. 3:8; Is 41:10; Ps 1:2-3

Prayer For Breakthrough

*The Lord has broken through my enemies before me, like a
breakthrough of water.* 2 Sam 5:20

Father, I come to You in the mighty Name of Jesus and declare
today that "You are the God of my Breakthrough". I approach
You today in confidence that if I ask anything according to
Your will You will hear my prayer and will answer me.

I declare that You are Jehovah Jireh, the God who provides. I
thank You that the Word of God declares that "I am blessed"
and that "all my needs are met according to Your riches in
glory".

I declare that breakthrough is coming in the way of provision,
deliverance, and opportunity. I thank You Lord that You are
opening doors of opportunity before me as I walk with You
believing that all things are possible.

I receive my breakthrough for provision, family salvation,
healing, deliverance, debt cancellation, financial increase, and
for a deeper understanding of Your ways and Your Word with
revelation knowledge and insight.

I declare that You are more than enough in all situations and
circumstances in my life. I trust You Father, to guide me
through the storms into the abundance that You have prepared
for me. You are faithful and true in all things. I Thank You
Lord that You are walking with me through all situations. Your
plans for me are to prosper and be in good health. I receive
today all that You have for me, In Jesus' Name.

I will keep my eyes fixed on You and Your Word that tells me that You are my healer, You are my Deliverer, You are my Strength and in Your presence is perfect peace.

No weapon formed against me shall prosper. When I look at my circumstances I will not allow doubt, fear and unbelief to overtake my mind. I will look to You and declare Your goodness and Your great grace that will carry me through to the breakthrough that You have prepared for me.

Thank You Lord for all You are about to do in my life. It is not the end but the beginning. I give You my life afresh today. I put my trust in You and You alone, Lord. Your great love overshadows me today and always.

Amen!

Study: Heb 4:16; Gen 22:14; Phil 4:19; I Cor 16:9; 2 Cor 9:8; Deut 31:8; 3 John 1:2; Is 26:3; Is 54:17; Matt 21:22; Ps 30:2

What I Have in Christ

I have the mind of Christ .... 1 Corinthians 2:16

I have the peace that passes all understanding .... Philippians 4:7

I have the Greater One living in me .... 1 John 4:4

I have the gift of righteousness .... Romans 5:17

I have the spirit of wisdom and revelation .... Ephesians 1:17-18

I have the power of the Holy Spirit to lay hands on the sick and see them recover, to cast out demons, to speak with new tongues ... Mark 16:17-18

I have power over all the power of the enemy, and nothing shall by any means harm me .... Luke 10:17-19

I have no lack for my God supplies all of my need .... Phil 4:19

I have the shield of faith which will quench all the fiery darts of the enemy .... Ephesians 6:16

I have an inheritance .... Romans 8:17

I have forgiveness for all my sin .... Ephesians 1:7

I have redemption from the curse of sin, sickness, and poverty ..... Gal 3:13

I have healing .... 1 Peter 2:24

I have strength .... Colossians 1:11

I have a spirit of power, love, and a sound mind .... 2 Tim 1:7

I have life through Christ who lives in me .... Gal 2:20

Chapter Eight

PRAYERS FOR OTHERS

Prayer for the Lost

Those who are wise shall shine like the brightness of the firmament, and those who turn many to righteousness like the stars forever and ever.
Dan 12:3

Precious and merciful Father, I uplift my friend to Your throne of grace. I thank You that You are longsuffering (extraordinarily patient), not desiring that any should perish, but that all should turn to repentance. Therefore, I ask that You grant repentance to my friend, so that he would come to know the truth, that he would come to his senses and escape out of the snare of the devil. Father, attract and draw my friend and give him the desire to come to Jesus. Holy Spirit, convince and convict him of sin, righteousness and judgment.

Lord, You have given me authority and power to trample upon serpents and scorpions and over all the power that the enemy possesses. I bind Satan and his demon forces, breaking every devilish assignment of the enemy against my friend, rendering them harmless and ineffective in Jesus' Name. I command Satan to take the blindfold off my friend's mind, and to open his ears, in Jesus' Name. I pray that the illuminating light of the gospel of the glory of Christ, the Messiah, may shine unto him, in the Name of Jesus Christ.

I pray, precious Father, that You will thrust forth laborers into Your harvest, and open doors of utterance to speak the mystery of Christ to my friend. I thank You that Your Word is alive and powerful, actively energized and sharper than any two-edged sword. It shall not return unto You void, but it will accomplish in my friend's life what You please, and prosper in the thing whereto You sent it. For You are alert and active, watching over Your Word to perform it.

I thank You that Your Word is a seed that will produce after its kind and that the entrance of Your Word into my friend's heart shall give light and understanding.

Now, Satan, and all demonic forces, in Jesus' Name, I forbid you to remove the seed of God's Word from my friend's heart. To this end I will pray in the Spirit and with my understanding also. In Jesus' Name.

Study: 2 Pet 3:9; 2 Tim 2:25; John 6.44; John 16:8; Luke 10:19; 2 Cor. 4:3-4; Matt 9:38; Col 4:3; Heb 4:12; Is 55:11; Jer 1:12; Gen 1:12; Ps 119:130; Mark 4:15; 1 Cor 14:15

Prayer for the Backslider

He who turns a sinner from the error of his way will save a soul from death and cover a multitude of sins. James 5:20

My Father, I uplift my friend to You, who has gone astray from Your path. I ask You to forgive his sins and grant him life. Restore him to right standing with You through the shed blood of Jesus and restore the joy of his salvation, renewing a right spirit within him. I pray that You will keep his heart soft before You at all times, so that You may continue to work in his life.

Father, through Jesus You have given my friend eternal life and I believe that he shall never lose it or perish or by any means be destroyed, for no one is able to snatch him out of Your hand. I pray that he will come to his senses now and escape the snare of the devil. Father, I know that You have seen his willful ways but You will heal him also, and will recompense him and restore comfort to him and to those who mourn for him.

Father, draw my friend to Yourself and grant repentance and restoration to him. I pray that the Word of God already planted in his heart will lead him when he sleeps and keep him when he wakes. I thank You Father, that all whom You have given (entrusted) to Jesus will come to Him and he who comes to Jesus will most certainly not be cast out. I pray also that my friend will not forsake or neglect to assemble with other believers, as is the habit of some people, but will fellowship with them, heeding their admonishing, warning, urging and encouraging, and all the more faithfully, since he knows the day is approaching.

Thank You, Father, that my friend is coming to You now, drawn by the Holy Spirit, and will serve You forever.

Study: Ps 51:10; John 10:28-29; 2 Tim 2:25; Is 57:18; John 12:32; Prov 6:22-23; John 6:37; Heb 10:25

For Those in Deception
or on Wrong Pathway

He leads me in the paths of righteousness for His Name's sake. Ps 23:3

Thank You Father, in Jesus' Name, that the Word of God leads my friend, keeps him when he sleeps and talks to him when he awakens. Your Word is a lamp unto his feet and a light unto his path. Lead him in the pathway of righteousness for Your Name's sake. Father, I thank You that You lead my friend in the way that he should go and counsel him with Your eye.

I pray that my friend hears the voice of the Good Shepherd and the voice of a stranger he will not hear. He is a son of God who is led by the Spirit of God. Thank You that the Spirit of truth teaches him and leads him into all truth. His pathway is like the light of dawn that shines more brightly and clearly until it reaches its full strength and glory unto that perfect day. In my friend's pathway is life and not death. He is God's own handiwork, created in Christ Jesus that he may do the works which You have predestined for him. He takes paths which You have prearranged and made ready for him to live. I bind every spirit of deception from his life in Jesus' Name.

Thank You for sending Your angel before my friend to keep him in the way and bring him to the place which You have prepared for him.

Study: Prov 6:22-24; Ps 119:105; Ps 23:3; Ps 32:8; John 10:4-6; John 16:13; Prov 4:18; Prov 12:28; Eph 2:10; Ex 23:20

How to Pray for Salvation

If you have never asked Jesus into your heart to be your Savior and Lord, pray this simple prayer with all your heart. After the prayer, sign your name and date it. Always look back to this moment when you became born again.

Father God, I believe Jesus Christ is the Son of God and that He died for my sins. I believe He rose from the dead on the third day for my salvation. I ask You to forgive my sins, for I am a sinner. I ask You, Lord Jesus, to come into my heart and cause me to be born again by the Holy Spirit. Thank You for eternal life. I believe I am saved and translated from darkness into the kingdom of light. Help me to study the Bible and do what You say in Your Word. Lead me to a good church that preaches the uncompromising Word of God, that I may grow and be used of You. In Jesus' Name.

I, _____

received Jesus Christ as my Lord and Savior today,

on _____.

I AM BORN AGAIN NOW!

Study: John 3:16-17; Rom 10:9-10; John 3:3; Col 1:13; 2 Tim 2:15; Heb 10:25

Receiving the Holy Spirit

If you have never been baptized in the Holy Spirit since you became a Christian, pray and ask the Father to fill you now. Firstly, read through the following scriptures to give you faith to believe:

Acts 2:37-39 / Acts 19:1-6

Luke 11:9-13 / Acts 10:44-48

Rest assured, based on these and other scriptures, that this wonderful gift of God is for YOU. It is for every believer. You must exercise faith, believing that it is yours for the asking, and that upon asking, God gives it. Then step out in faith and begin to speak in new tongues.

Dear Father, I am Your obedient child. I ask You now to fill me to overflowing with Your precious Holy Spirit. I receive Him now as a gift and by faith I speak with new tongues in Jesus' Name.

Now begin to speak out, not in English, but in your new language. Make your new language a daily part of your prayer life.

Who I am In Christ

I am a child of God .... John 1:12

I am a friend of Jesus .... John 15:15

I am justified and redeemed .... Romans 3:24

I am not condemned .... Romans 8:1

I am accepted .... Romans 15:7

I am a new creation .... 2 Corinthians 5:17

I am the righteousness of God .... 2 Corinthians 5:21

I am set free .... Galatians 5:1

I am blessed with every spiritual blessing in the heavenly places ....
.... Ephesians 1:3

I am chosen, holy, and blameless .... Ephesians 1:4

I am sealed with the Holy Spirit of promise .... Ephesians 1:13

I am seated in the heavenly places with Christ .... Ephesians 2:6

I am God's workmanship .... Ephesians 2:10

I am a member of Christ's body .... Ephesians 3:6

I am a citizen of heaven .... Philippians 3:20

I am complete in Christ .... Colossians 2:10

I am chosen of God, and I am holy and beloved .... Colossians 3:12

I am an overcomer .... Revelation 12:11

I am an ambassador for Christ .... 2 Corinthians 5:20

I am the head and not the tail; I am above only and not beneath .. Deut 28:13

I am the light of the world ....Matthew 5:14

I am forgiven of all my sins and washed in the Blood ....Ephesians 1:7

I am greatly loved by God ....Ephesians 2:4

I am firmly rooted, built up, established in my faith and overflowing with gratitude ....Colossians 2:7

I am a doer of the Word ....James 1:22-25

I am far from oppression, and fear does not come near me ......Isaiah 54:14

TESTIMONY

Cancer Healed Using Hazel Hill's
Praying God's Word Book

By Ray Duff

During a routine medical examination in September 1998, I was diagnosed with lymphoma cancer and was given three months to live. Three other doctors confirmed the diagnosis. Thanks to God for His supernatural gift of faith, I was able to break the news to my family without fear, knowing I would receive a miracle from God.

Two weeks later, we held our regular prayer meeting with two other couples. When we arrived, I was surprised to see that everyone was sick. We started praising God when the Holy Spirit took over and led me to pray for everyone. My friend Jack then got up, took Dr. Hazel Hill's book, "Praying God's Word", put his hand on my abdomen and prayed the prayer about cancer.

The next day, my doctor examined me to localize the tumour and decide on treatment. He said: "Ray, I don't know what's happening, I can't find it". I told him "Praise God, Jesus healed me". Several tests were done to find the tumour; all tests confirmed that there was no trace of cancer in my body. Two other doctors confirmed this final diagnosis.

As a result of my miraculous healing, ten of my family members received Christ!! Praise the Lord!

Books

Adventure, Romance & Revival
By Drs. George & Hazel Hill

This is the autobiography of Drs. George & Hazel Hill; an ordinary couple doing extraordinary exploits for God. Adventure, Romance & Revival traces the history of this couple from their childhood; conversion; to the founding of Victory Churches International, a ministry with churches, Bible Colleges, and orphanages in over 40 countries around the world.

The Husband and Wife Ministry Team
By Dr. Hazel Hill

God's plan is for husbands and wives to flow together in ministry. In this book Dr. Hazel Hill provides practical principles for effectiveness; discusses different husband and wife ministry teams, and challenges couples to fulfill God's purpose for their lives.

The Interceding Christian
By Drs. George and Hazel Hill

God is raising up a people who know their God and who are able to do exploits in His Name. This book will help you understand the spirit realm and teach you how to be an effective intercessor.

Interceding Christian Workbook is also available

Releasing Women to Minister
By Dr. Hazel Hill

It is like the story of Mary in the Bible. Even though women have been denied ministry in our churches, for centuries they have gone and wept over and anointed hurting humanity because of their love for Jesus. Jesus has received their ministry. Will you?

Planting Healthy Growing Churches
By Dr. George S. Hill & Bradley T. Dewar

This book takes us far beyond theory and offers the kind of practical wisdom that can only be gained from being personally involved in numerous church plants. It is a prayerfully written, time-tested handbook for church-planters and their organizations to refer to again and again.

To order more copies of **Praying God's Word** or more books by Drs. George and Hazel Hill please visit:

www.victorybookstore.org or www.amazon.com

Or write:
Victory Churches International
10623 West Valley Road SW
CALGARY, AB
T3B 5T2

Or call:
1-403-286-8337

Or email:
office@victoryint.org

Victory Bible Colleges International

International Campus – Calgary, Alberta

- ❖ One Year Certificate, Two Year Diploma, Three Year Diploma
- ❖ Four Year Bachelor of Theology, Christian Counseling Degree
- ❖ Graduate Studies, including Masters and Doctorate Degree Programs
- ❖ Correspondence Courses
- ❖ Live-in accommodation in our 50,000 sq ft Victory Village complex
- ❖ Music and Theatre Arts programs
- ❖ Television, recording and multimedia training

10623 West Valley Road SW
Calgary, AB T3B 5T2
Phone: 403-286-8337 Fax: 403-286-8335
Email: office@vbci.org   Website: www.vbci.org

Educating the Head – Impacting the Heart – Empowering the Hands

Many full-time ministry opportunities for graduates through Victory Churches International